Webster's New World™

Best Book of

Aphorisms

Auriel Douglas

Michael Strumpf

Webster's New World

New York

**WEBSTER'S
NEW WORLD**

Simon & Schuster, Inc.
Gulf + Western Building
One Gulf + Western Plaza
New York, NY 10023

DISTRIBUTED BY PRENTICE HALL TRADE

Manufactured in the United States of America

1 2 3 4 5 6 7 8 9 10

Library of Congress Cataloging-in-Publication Data

Douglas, Auriel.
    Webster's new world best book of aphorisms /
Auriel Douglas, Michael Strumpf.
        p.   cm.
    Includes index.
    ISBN 0-13-947128-6
    1. Aphorisms and apothegms.   I. Strumpf,
Michael.   II. Title.
PN6271.D68   1989   88-37519
808.88'2—dc19   CIP

Introduction

The purpose of this book is to highlight words that can help the reader reinforce speeches, underline important points, and perhaps deliver a brilliant illumination of some obscure point.

These words spoken by names—some familiar, some strange—are an eternal legacy; when they were originally spoken or written, the author certainly had little idea that his/her verbiage would last into eternity. Yet here they are, helping to guide us either by solving problems or providing inspiration.

These aphorisms are bright, pithy, and usable. Delivered by the likes of Goethe, Wilde, Bierce, Butler, Russell, Johnson, Baudelaire, and Vauvenargues, they serve to guide us when we are incapable of providing our own wisdom to solve a dilemma, spark a conversation, or fascinate an audience. Their uses are limitless.

The authors hope that the selection will meet the reader's needs and ultimately give pleasure, wisdom, and inspiration, and that this book will be a welcome addition to all libraries.

On the following page is a list of the many different classes of sayings and their definitions.

Adage: An old saying that has been popularly accepted as a truth.

Anecdote: A little known, entertaining fact of history or biography. A short, entertaining account of some happening, usually personal or biographical.

Aphorism: A concise statement of a principle, a short, pointed sentence expressing a wise or clever observation or a general truth.

Apothegm: A short, pithy saying.

Axiom: A statement universally accepted as true, an established principle or law of a science, art, etc.

Bromide: A trite saying or statement. Synonym: platitude.

Cliche: An expression or idea that has become trite.

Dictum: A statement or saying; specifically, a formal statement of fact, opinion, principle, etc., or of one's will or judgment; a pronouncement.

Maxim: A concisely expressed principle or rule of conduct, or a statement of a general truth. Synonym: saying.

Motto: A word, phrase, or sentence chosen as expressive of the goals or ideals of a nation or group and inscribed on a seal, banner, coin, etc.

Proverb: A short saying in common use that strikingly expresses some obvious truth or familiar experience. Synonyms: adage, maxim.

Quip: A witty or sarcastic remark or reply.

Saying: Something said. An adage, proverb, or maxim; the simple, direct term for any pithy expression of wisdom or truth.

Saw: An old homely saying that is well worn by repetition.

Truism: A statement the truth of which is obvious or well known; commonplace. Synonym: platitude.

Ability

Talent without genius isn't much, but genius without talent is nothing whatever.

—Paul Valéry

They are able because they think they are able.

—Virgil

To do great work, a man must be very idle as well as very industrious.

—Samuel Butler

We succeed in enterprises which demand the positive qualities we possess, but we excel in those which also make use of our defects.

—Alexis de Tocqueville

From such crooked wood as that which man is made of, nothing straight can be fashioned.

—Edward Hand

Ability is commonly found to consist mainly in a big degree of solemnity.

—Ambrose Bierce

1

Talent is an adornment; an adornment is also a concealment.

—Anon.

Ability is nothing without opportunity.

—Napoleon

To measure up to all that is demanded of him, a man must overestimate his capacities.

—Johann Wolfgang von Goethe

One machine can do the work of fifty ordinary men. No machine can do the work of one extraordinary man.

—Elbert Hubbard

See ACCOMPLISHMENT, ACHIEVEMENT, JOBS, WORK

Accomplishment

Could we know what men are most apt to remember, we might know what they are most apt to do.

—Lord Halifax

For a thing to remain undone nothing more is needed than to think it done.

—*Baltasar Gracián*

Those that have done nothing in life are not qualified to judge of those that have done little.

—*Samuel Johnson*

There is always a multitude of reasons both in favor of doing a thing and against doing it. The art of debate lies in presenting them. The art of life lies in neglecting ninety-nine hundredths of them.

—*Anon.*

No task is a long one but the task on which one dare not start. It becomes a nightmare.

—*Charles Baudelaire*

Never undertake anything unless you have the heart to ask Heaven's blessing on your undertaking.

—*Georg Christoph Lichtenberg*

The test of a vocation is the love of the drudgery it involves.

—*Anon.*

The reward of a thing well done, is to have done it.

—*Ralph Waldo Emerson*

Men despise great projects when they do not feel themselves capable of great successes.

—*Marquis de Vauvenargues*

Nothing will ever be attempted if all possible objections must be first overcome.

—*Samuel Johnson*

We have got but one life here. It pays, no matter what comes after it, to try and do things, to accomplish things in this life and not merely to have a soft and pleasant time.

—*Theodore Roosevelt*

See ABILITY, ACHIEVEMENT, JOBS, WORK

Achievement

We act as though it were our mission to bring about the triumph of truth, but our mission is only to fight for it.

—*Blaise Pascal*

Every calling is great when greatly pursued.

—*Oliver Wendell Holmes*

The only thing some people do is get older.

—*E. W. Howe*

Life is at best only a children's game. Yet the game must be played conscientiously.

—*Yukichi*

The world is moving so fast these days that the man who says it can't be done is generally interrupted by someone doing it.

—*Elbert Hubbard*

The man who is born with a talent which he has meant to use finds his greatest happiness in using it.

—*Johann Wolfgang von Goethe*

If you cannot work with love but only with distaste it is better that you should leave your work and sit at the gates of the temple and take alms of those who work with joy.

—*Kahlil Gibran*

It is, no doubt, an immense advantage to have done nothing, but one should not abuse it.

—*Antoine de Rivarol*

This is the true joy in life, the being used for a purpose recognized by yourself as a mighty one, the being thoroughly worn out before you are thrown on the scrap heap, the being a force of nature instead of a feverish selfish little clod of ailments and grievances complaining that the world will not devote itself to making you happy.

—*George Bernard Shaw*

Discard the old maxim, "Do not get others to do what you can do yourself." My motto is, do not do that which others can do as well.

—*Booker T. Washington*

Perseverance is a great element of success; if you only knock long enough and loud enough at the gate you are sure to wake up somebody.

—*Henry Wadsworth Longfellow*

There is no such thing as a great talent without great will-power.

—*Honoré de Balzac*

Between vague wavering Capability and fixed indubitable Performance, what a difference!

—*Thomas Carlyle*

The youth gets together his materials to build a bridge to the moon, or, perchance, a palace or temple on the earth, and, at length, the middle aged man concludes to build a woodshed with them.

—*Henry David Thoreau*

See ABILITY, ACCOMPLISHMENT, JOBS, WORK

Acting

Acting is not an important job in the scheme of things. Plumbing is.

—*Spencer Tracy*

I never said that all actors are cattle; what I said was that all actors should be treated like cattle.

—*Alfred Hitchcock*

What acting means is that you've got to get out of your own skin.

—*Katherine Hepburn*

Act singly, and what you have already done singly will justify you now.

—*Ralph Waldo Emerson*

We wear the robes that we have designed for ourself, and then act out other people's fantasies.

—*Laurence Olivier*

An actor is a sculptor who carves in snow.

—*Barret-Booth*

You can pick out the actors by the glazed look that comes into their eyes when the conversation wanders away from themselves.

—*Michael Wilding*

Acting is just one big bag of tricks.

—*Laurence Olivier*

You say, "Let's get it done real," but acting is just one version of the unreal after another.

—*Jack Nicholson*

Show me a great actor, and I'll show you a lousy husband. Show me a great actress, and you've seen the devil.

—*W. C. Fields*

Some of the greatest love affairs I've known involved one actor, unassisted.

—*Wilson Mizner*

See HOLLYWOOD, FILMS, TALENT, TELEVISION

Action

There enters into all human action more luck than judgment.

—*André Gide*

To act responsibly, you have to take leaps without being sane.

—*Daniel Ellsberg*

A person has to be busy to stay alive.

—*Maxwell Anderson*

Enthusiasm finds the opportunities, and energy makes the most of them.

—*Henry Hoskins*

I believe in living life dangerously; I think a lot of others do too.

—Prince Charles

The absence of alternatives clears the mind marvelously.

—Henry Kissinger

What the hell . . . you might be right; you might be wrong, but don't just avoid.

—Katherine Hepburn

Nothing is so exhausting as indecision, and nothing so futile.

—Bertrand Russell

It's easier to fight for one's principles than to live up to them.

—Adlai Stevenson

Act only on that maxim through which you can at the same time will that it should become a universal law.

—Immanuel Kant

He who desires, but acts not, breeds pestilence.

—William Blake

Behind many acts that many thought ridiculous, there lie many wise and weighty motives.

—*François de La Rochefoucauld*

All the fun is locking horns with impossibilities.

—*Claus Oldenburg*

What the world needs is some "do give a damn pills."

—*William Meninger*

See CONFIDENCE AND SUCCESS

Adolescence

In America, the young are always ready to give to those that are older than themselves the full benefits of their inexperience.

—*Oscar Wilde*

A simple child,
That lightly draws its breath,
And feels its life in every limb,
What should it know of death?

—*William Wordsworth*

My salad days,
When I was green in judgment, cold in blood, to say as I
said then.

—*William Shakespeare: Anthony and Cleopatra*

Then come kiss me, sweet and twenty, youth's a stuff will
not endure.

—*William Shakespeare: Sonnets*

Young fellows are tempted by girls; men who are thirty
years old are tempted by gold; when they are forty years
old, they are tempted by honor and glory, and those
who are sixty years old, say to themselves, "What a
pious man I have become."

—*Martin Luther*

Consider well the proportions of things. It is better to be
a young June bug than an old bird of paradise.

—*Anon.*

The childhood shews the man as morning shews the day.

—*John Milton*

I remember my youth and the feeling that will never
come back any more, the feeling that I could last
forever, outlast the sea, the earth, and all men.

—*Joseph Conrad*

Crabbed age and youth cannot live together; Youth is full of pleasance, age is full of care. Youth like summer morn; age like winter weather; youth like summer brave; age like winter bear; youth is full of sport; age's breath is short; youth is nimble; age is lame; youth is hot, and old age is weak and cold; youth is wild, and age is tame; age, I do abhor thee; youth, I do adore thee.

—William Shakespeare

Maybe more youngsters would stay home nights if they weren't afraid to stay alone in the house.

—Herbert Prochnow

Old places and old persons in their turn, when spirit dwells in them, have an intrinsic vitality of which youth is incapable, precisely, the balance and wisdom that come from long perspectives and broad foundations.

—George Santayana

See AGE, CHILDREN

Advertising

Advertising is the art of making whole lies out of half truths.

—Edgar Shoaff

Advertisements contain the only truth to be relied on in the newspaper.

—Thomas Jefferson

Let advertisers spend the same amount of money improving their product as they do on advertising, and they wouldn't have to advertise it.

—Will Rogers

You can tell the ideals of a nation by its advertisements.

—Norman Douglas

Invention is the mother of necessity.

—Thorstein Veblen

Advertising may be described as the science of arresting the human intelligence long enough to get money from it.

—Stephen Leacock

Advertising is the rattling of a stick inside a swill bucket.

—George Orwell

Advertising is legalized lying.

—H. G. Wells

Advice

Don't give a woman advice; one should never give a woman anything she can't wear in the evening.

—Oscar Wilde

A good scare is worth more to a man than good advice.

—E. W. Howe

They have a right to censure that have a heart to help.

—William Penn

It is always a silly thing to give advice, but to give good advice is fatal.

—Oscar Wilde

In giving advice, I advise you, be short.

—Horace

"Be yourself" is about the worst advice you can give to people.

—Tom Masson

I have found to best way to give advice to your children is to find out what they want and then advise them to do it.

—*Harry Truman*

Old people like to give good advice, as solace for no longer being able to provide bad example.

—*François de La Rochefoucauld*

To ask for advice is, in nine cases out of ten, to tout for flattery.

—*Anon.*

See CRITICISM

Afterlife

We feel and know that we are eternal.

—*Baruch Spinoza*

Is there another life? Shall I awake and find this all a dream? There must be; we cannot be created for this type of suffering.

—*John Keats*

Nothing is eternal, alas, except eternity.

—*Paul Fort*

God will often say to us; "You are not in Heaven for fun!"

—*Jules Renard*

I can believe anything, but the justice of this world does not give me a very reassuring idea of the justice in the next. I am very much afraid that God will go on blundering; he will receive the wicked in paradise and hurl the good into hell.

—*Jules Renard*

Ah, but a man's reach should exceed his grasp,
Or what's a heaven for?

—*Robert Browning*

God is growing bitter. He envies man his mortality.

—*Jacques Rigaut*

Parting is all we know of heaven,
And all we need of hell.

—*Emily Dickinson*

After your death you will be what you were before your birth.

—*Arthur Schopenhauer*

Heaven goes by favor, if it went by merit, you would stay out, and your dog would go in.

—Mark Twain

The heavens declare the glory of God; and the firmament showeth his handiwork.

—Psalms 19:1

To reach the port of heaven, we must sail sometimes with the wind and sometimes against it—but we must sail, and not drift, nor lie at anchor.

—Oliver Wendel Holmes

Good Americans, when they die, go to Paris.

—Thomas Gold Appleton

When bad Americans die, they go to America.

—Oscar Wilde

Many might go to heaven with half the labor they go to hell.

—Ralph Waldo Emerson

What they do in heaven, we are ignorant of. What they do not do we are told expressly.

—Jonathan Swift

What a man misses most in heaven is company.

—*Mark Twain*

See BIBLE, GOD, HELL

Age

For time it is, age has great advantages; experience and wisdom come with age. Men may be old outrun, but not outwit.

—*Geoffrey Chaucer*

Old age is not so bad when you consider the alternative.

—*Maurice Chevalier*

Dawn comes slowly, but dusk is rapid.

—*Alice B. Toklas*

We do not count a man's years until he has nothing else to count.

—*Ralph Waldo Emerson*

Getting married and getting old are the two things that save everybody's ass.

—*Cher*

When I was young, I used to say good-natured things, and nobody listened to me. Now that I am old, I say ill-natured things, and everybody listens to me.

—Samuel Rogers

Old men are children for a second time.

—Aristophanes

Age is deformed, youth unkind. We scorn their bodies, they, our mind.

—Anon.

Forty is the old age of youth; fifty is the youth of old age.

—Victor Hugo

We look forward to a disorderly, vigorous, unhonored, and disreputable old age.

—Don Marquis

Middle age is the time when a man is always thinking that in a week or two he will feel as good as ever.

—Don Marquis

No wise man ever wished to be younger.

—Jonathan Swift

If youth but knew, if old age but could.

—Henri Estienne

Grow old along with me!
The best is yet to be . . .

—Robert Browning

A man of sixty has spent twenty years in bed and over three years in eating.

—Arnold Bennett

Old age is the night of life, as night is the old age of the day. Still night is full of magnificence and, for many, it is more brilliant than the day.

—Ann Sophie Swetchine

I am not young enough to know everything.

—Oscar Wilde

Unfortunately, man never gets too old or too experienced to be stupid in some new way.

—Herbert Prochnow

No man is so old as to think he cannot live one more year.

—Cicero

For the unlearned, old age is winter; for the learned it is the season of the harvest.

—Talmud

It is magnificent to grow old if one keeps young.

—*Harry Emerson Fosdick*

There are few things that are so unwillingly given up, even in advanced age as the supposition that we have still the power of ingratiating ourselves with the fair sex.

—*Samuel Johnson*

Youth had been a habit of hers for so long that she could not part with it.

—*Rudyard Kipling*

The longer thread of life we spin, the more occasion still to sin.

—*Robert Herrick*

I think age is a very high price to pay for maturity.

—*Tom Stoppard*

Nothing so dates a man as to decry the younger generation.

—*Adlai Stevenson*

At fifty, a man's real life begins. He has acquired upon which to achieve, received from which to give, learned from which to teach, clearned upon which to build.

—*Derek Bok*

The best years are the forties. After fifty, a man begins to deteriorate, but in the forties he is at the maximum of his villainy.

—H. Mencken

Old age puts more wrinkles in our minds than on our faces, and we never, or rarely, see a soul that in growing old does not come to smell sour and musty. Man grows and dwindles in his entirety.

—Ashley Montague

Wounds heal and become scars, but scars grow with us.

—Stanislaw Lec

Old age takes away from us what we have inherited and gives us what we have earned.

—Gerald Brenan

To be adult is to be alone.

—Jean Rostand

Old age is a shipwreck.

—Charles De Gaulle

Setting a good example for your children takes all the fun out of middle age.

—William Feather

Men are like wine; some turn to vinegar, but the best improve with age.

—Pope John XXIII

There is nothing sadder than an old hipster.

—Lenny Bruce

Anyone can get old; all you have to do is to live long enough.

—Groucho Marx

As you grow older, you'll find the only things you regret are the things you didn't do.

—Zachary Scott

See LIFE

Alcohol

A man is never drunk if he can lay on the floor without holding on.

—Joe E. Lewis

I have always taken more out of alcohol than alcohol has taken out of me.

> —*Winston Churchill*

In wine, there is truth.

> —*Pliny the Elder*

The worst thing about some men is that when they are drunk they are sober.

> —*William Butler Yeats*

Of all vices, drinking is the most incompatible with greatness.

> —*Sir Walter Scott*

I always wake up at the crack of ice.

> —*Joe E. Lewis*

See DESPERATION, EMPTINESS

Alimony

She cried and the judge wiped her tears with my checkbook.

—*Tommy Manville*

Alimony is like buying oats for a dead horse

—*Arthur Baer*

You never realize how short a month is until you pay alimony.

—*John Barrymore*

See MARRIAGE, DIVORCE

Ambition

I had ambition not only to go farther than any man had been before, but as far as it was possible for a man to go.

—*Joseph Cook*

Everybody sets out to do something, and everybody does something, but no one does what he sets out to do.

—*George Moore*

Ours is a world where people don't know what they want and are willing to go through hell to get it.

—*Don Marquis*

One can never consent to creep when one feels an impulse to soar.

—*Helen Keller*

Ambition is like hunger; it obeys no law but its appetite.

—*Herbert Shaw*

Keep away from people who try to belittle your ambitions. Small people always do that, but the really great make you feel that you, too, can become great.

—*Mark Twain*

By working faithfully eight hours per day, you may eventually get to be a boss and work twelve hours a day.

—*Robert Frost*

See SUCCESS, WORK

America is the only country where you buy a lifetime supply of aspirin and use it up in two weeks.

—*John Barrymore*

Americans are like a rich father who wishes he knew how to give his sons the hardships that made him rich.

—*Robert Frost*

The American people never carry an umbrella. They prepare to walk in eternal sunshine.

—*Al Smith*

Intellectually, I know that America is no better than any other country. Emotionally, I know she is better than every other country.

—*Sinclair Lewis*

Only Americans can hurt America.

—*Dwight D. Eisenhower*

America is a large friendly dog in a small room. Every time it wags its tail, it knocks over a chair.

—*Arnold Toynbee*

America had often been discovered before Columbus,
but it had always been hushed up.

—*Oscar Wilde*

A man who thinks of himself as belonging to a particular
national group in America has not yet become an
American.

—*Woodrow Wilson*

I don't know why vigor went out of America and why a
con man blandness replaced it.

—*Ben Hecht*

See ENGLAND

Ancestry

I don't know who my grandfather was; I am much more
concerned to know what his grandson will be.

—*Abraham Lincoln*

If you cannot get rid of the family skeleton, you may as
well make it dance.

—*George Bernard Shaw*

Snobs talk as if they had forgotten their ancestors.

—*Horatio Alger*

The sharp thorn often produces delicate roses.

—*Ovid*

My folks didn't come over on the *Mayflower*, but they were there to meet the boat.

—*Will Rogers*

Genealogist: one who traces back your family as far as your money will go.

—*Oscar Wilde*

She is descended from a long line her mother listened to.

—*Gypsy Rose Lee*

There is no king who has not had a slave amongst his ancestors, and no slave who has not had a king among his.

—*Helen Keller*

Once in every half century, at longest, a family should be merged into the great obscure mass of humanity and forget all about its ancestors.

—*Nathaniel Hawthorne*

None of us can boast about the morality of our ancestors. The records do not show that Adam and Eve were married.

—E. W. Howe

See FAMILY, PARENTS

Anger

Anger blows out the lamp of the mind.

—Robert Ingersoll

Never forget what a man has said to you when he was angry.

—Henry Ward Beecher

When angry, count four; when very angry, swear.

—Mark Twain

Anger is never without an argument, but seldom with a good one.

—Lord Halifax

How much more grievous are the consequences of anger than the causes of it.

—*Marcus Aurelius*

A hurtful act is the transference to others of the degradation which we bear in ourselves.

—*Simone Weil*

Think when you are enraged at anyone, what would probably become your sentiments should he die during the dispute.

—*William Shenstone*

A contest between relatives is usually conducted with more acrimony than a dispute with strangers.

—*Anon.*

See DISPUTE, EMOTION

Animals

We hope that when the insects take over the world, they will remember with gratitude how we took them along on our picnics.

—*Billy Vaughn*

Men are the only animals that devote themselves, day in and day out to making one another happy.

—*H. L. Mencken*

I have always thought of a dog lover as a dog that was in love with another dog.

—*James Thurber*

Mankind differs from the animals only by a little, and most people throw that away.

—*Confucius*

All animals except man know that the ultimate in life is to enjoy it.

—*Samuel Butler*

All animals are equal, but some animals are more equal than others.

—*George Orwell*

Animals have these advantages over man: they have no theologians to instruct them; their funerals cost them nothing, and no one starts lawsuits over their wills.

—*Voltaire*

I distrust camels, and anyone else who can go a week without a drink.

—*Joe E. Lewis*

If modern civilised man had to keep the animals he eats, the number of vegetarians would rise astronomically.

—*Christian Morgenstern*

Behind each beautiful wild fur, there is an ugly story. It is a brutal, bloody and barbaric story. The animal is not killed, it is tortured. I don't think a fur coat is worth it.

—*Mary Tyler Moore*

See CATS, DOGS

The Arts

What garlic is to salad, insanity is to art.

—*Augustus Saint-Gaudens*

Art happens—no hovel is safe from it, no prince may depend upon it, the vastest intelligence cannot bring it about.

—*James McNeill Whistler*

The painter should not paint what he sees, but what will be seen.

—*Paul Valéry*

Immature poets imitate; mature poets steal.

—*T. S. Eliot*

A poet looks at the world as a man looks at a woman.

—*Wallace Stevens*

It is as easy to dream a book as it is hard to write one.

—*Honoré de Balzac*

The important thing is not what the author, or any artist, had in mind to begin with but at what point he decided to stop.

—*D. W. Harding*

For art to exist, for any sort of aesthetic activity or perception to exist, a certain physiological precondition is indispensable; intoxication.

—*Friedrich Wilhelm Nietzsche*

I think having land and not ruining it is the most beautiful art that anybody could ever want to own.

—*Andy Warhol*

Publicity often seems to be about all that is left of the arts.

—*Igor Stravinsky*

Art is I; science is we.

—*Claude Bernard*

Of all lies, art is the least untrue.

—*Gustave Flaubert*

Bad artists always admire each other's work.

—*Oscar Wilde*

Any authentic work of art must start an argument between an artist and his audience.

—*Rebecca West*

A primitive artist is an amateur whose work sells.

—*Grandma Moses*

If it is art, it is not for all, and if it is for all, it is not art.

—*Arnold Schoenberg*

Art is uncompromising, and life is full of compromises.

—*Günther Grass*

The rule in the art world is you cater to the masses, or you kowtow to the elite; you can't have both.

—*Ben Hecht*

Art is nature speeded up, and God slowed down.

—*M. Chazal*

Life is more important than art; that's what makes art important.

—*James Baldwin*

To do easily what is difficult for others is the mark of talent. To do what is impossible for talent is the mark of genius.

—*Henri Amiel*

Only a person with a Best Seller mind can write Best Sellers.

—*Aldous Huxley*

See BOOKS, MUSIC

Authors

Your manuscript is both good and original, but the part that is good is not original, and the part that is original is not good.

—*Samuel Johnson*

It took me fifteen years to discover I had no talent for writing, but I couldn't give it up because by that time I was too famous.

—*Nathaniel Benchley*

No one can write decently who is distrustful of the reader's intelligence or whose attitude is patronizing.

—*E. B. White*

I love being a writer. What I can't stand is the paperwork.

—*Anon.*

Literary success of any enduring kind is made by refusing to do what publishers want, by refusing to write what the public wants, by refusing to accept any popular standard, by refusing to write anything to order.

—*Anon.*

From the moment I picked your book up, to the moment I laid it down, I was convulsed with laughter; some day I intend to read it.

—*Groucho Mark*

A pin has as much head on it as some authors and a good deal more point.

—*George Prentice*

Writing is the only profession where no one considers you ridiculous if you earn no money.

—*Jules Renard*

The earliest poets and authors made fools wise. Modern authors try to make wise men fools.

—*Joseph Joubert*

The secret of popular writing is never to put more on a given page than the common reader can lap off it with no strain whatsoever on his habitually slack attention.

—*Ezra Pound*

Almost anyone can be an author; the business is to collect money and fame from this state of being.

—*A. A. Milne*

Only a small minority of authors overwrite themselves. Most of the good and the tolerable ones do not write enough.

—*Arnold Bennett*

With sixty staring me in the face, I have developed imflammation of the sentence structure and a definite hardening of the paragraphs.

—*James Thurber*

The author who speaks about his own books is almost as bad as the mother who talks about her own children.

—*Benjamin Disraeli*

Writing is not a profession but a vocation of unhappiness.

—*Georges Simenon*

Everything goes by the board: honor, pride, decency, security, happiness, all, to get the book written. If a writer has to rob his mother, he will not hesitate . . .

—*William Faulkner*

You must not suppose, because I am a man of letters, that I never tried to earn an honest living.

—*George Bernard Shaw*

Writing a book is not as tough as it is to haul thirty-five people around the country and sweat like a horse five nights a week.

—*Bette Midler*

See BOOKS, EDUCATION, LEARNING, LITERATURE, WORDS

Bachelor

Bachelors know more about women than married men. If they didn't they'd be married too.

—*H. L. Mencken*

Call no man unhappy until he's married.

—*Socrates*

A bachelor is one who thinks one can live as cheap as two.

—*E. Ridley*

A bachelor never quite gets over the idea that he is a thing of beauty and a boy forever.

—*H. Rowland*

The only good husbands stay bachelors; they are too considerate to get married.

—*Finley Peter Dunne*

The world must be peopled. When I said I would die a bachelor, I did not think I should live till I were married.

—*William Shakespeare: Much Ado About Nothing*

By persistently remaining single, a man converts himself into a permanent public temptation.

—*Oscar Wilde*

It is a truth universally acknowledged, that a single man in possession of a good fortune, must be in want of a wife.

—*Jane Austen*

See MARRIAGE

One of the difficult tasks in this world is to convince a woman that even a bargain costs money.

—*E. W. Howe*

Marriage is a bargain. And somebody has to get the worst of a bargain.

—*Helen Rowland*

A woman will buy anything she thinks the store is losing money on.

—*Kin Hubbard*

What costs little is little worth.

—*Baltasar Gracián*

A bargain is something you can't use but which is so cheap you can't afford not to buy it.

—*Herbert Prochnow*

Beauty

We live only to discover beauty. All else is a form of waiting.

—*Kahlil Gibran*

Beauty without grace is a hook without bait.

—*Ninon de L'Enclos*

The saying that beauty is but skin deep is but a skin deep saying.

—*Herbert Spencer*

The copy of a beautiful thing is always an ugly thing. It is an act of cowardice in admiration of an act of energy.

—*Rémy de Gourmont*

The inappropriate cannot be beautiful.

—*Frank Lloyd Wright*

People who are very beautiful make their own laws.

—*Vivien Leigh*

Remember that the most beautiful things in the world are the most useless: peacocks and lilies for instance.

—*John Ruskin*

Few girls are as well shaped as a good horse.

—*Christopher Morley*

In the eyes of a lover, pockmarks are dimples.

—*Anon.*

Everything beautiful has its moments and then passes away.

—*Luis Cernuda*

A beautiful woman is paradise for the eyes, hell for soul, and purgatory for the purse.

—*Nicolas Chamfort*

The only way to behave to a woman is to make love to her if she is pretty and to someone else if she is plain.

—*Oscar Wilde*

A beautiful woman with a brain is like a beautiful woman with a club foot.

—*Bernard Cornfeld*

Beauty is how you feel inside, and it reflects in your eyes. It is not something physical.

—*Sophia Loren*

There are many beautiful things, but the silent beauty of a flower surpasses them all.

—*S. Teshigahara*

Behavior

There are some people who are very resourceful at being resourceful and who apparently feel that the best way to make friends is to do something terrible and then to make amends.

—*Ogden Nash*

He who takes a stand is often wrong, but he who fails to take a stand is always wrong.

—*Anon.*

Nothing prevents our being natural as the desire to seem so.

—*Arthur Schopenhauer*

Few things are harder to put up with than the annoyance of a good example.

—*Mark Twain*

Therefore all things whatsoever ye would that men should do to you, do ye even so to them . . .

—*Matthew 7:12*

Almost all absurdity of conduct arises from the imitation of those whom we cannot resemble.

—*Samuel Johnson*

No man is rich enough to buy back his past.

—*Oscar Wilde*

We are all capable of evil thoughts, but only rarely of evil deeds, We can all do good deeds but very few of us can think good thoughts.

—*Brese*

We think in generalities, but we live in detail.

—*Alfred North Whitehead*

See CHARACTER, MAN, SELF

Believing

Men who borrow their opinions can never repay their debts.

—*Lord Halifax*

There is nothing that fear nor hope does not make men believe.

—*Marquis de Vauvenargues*

What a man thinks of himself, that it is which determines, or rather indicates, his fate.

—*Henry David Thoreau*

Prejudice is never easy unless it can pass itself off for reason.

—*William Hazlitt*

Nothing is more dangerous than an idea, when it's the only one we have.

—*Alain*

The more faithfully you listen to the voice within you, the better you will hear what is sounding outside. And only he who listens can speak.

—*Dag Hammarskjold*

Many a time I have wanted to stop talking and find out what I really believed.

—*Walter Lippman*

I can believe anything provided it is incredible.

—*Oscar Wilde*

Convictions are more dangerous enemies of truth than lies.

—*Fredrich Wilhelm Nietzsche*

Irrationally held truths may be more harmful than reasoned errors.

—*Thomas Henry Huxley*

Those who never retract their opinions love themselves more than they love the truth.

—*Joseph Joubert*

With most men, unbelief in one thing springs from blind belief in another.

—*Georg Christoph Lichtenberg*

See BIBLE, CHRISTIANITY, CONVICTIONS, GOD, TRUST

A knowledge of the Bible without a college course is more valuable than a college course without the Bible.

—*William Lyon Phelps*

In all my perplexities and distresses, the Bible has never failed to give me light and strength.

—*Anon.*

That book, sir, is the rock on which our republic rests.

—*Andrew Jackson*

The Bible tells us to love our neighbours and also to love our enemies, probably because they are generally the same people.

—*G. K. Chesterton*

It is impossible to enslave mentally or socially a Bible reading people. The principles of the Bible are the groundwork of human freedom.

—*Horace Greeley*

Scriptures are the sacred books of our holy religion, as distinguished from the false and profane writings on which all other faiths are based.

—*Ambrose Bierce*

The scriptures teach us the best way of living, the noblest way of suffering, and the most comfortable way of dying.

—*John Flavel*

The inspiration of the Bible depends on the ignorance of the gentleman who reads it.

—*Robert Ingersoll*

I have read the Bible carefully and if Bob Ingersoll isn't in hell, God is a liar and the Bible isn't worth the paper it is printed on.

—*Billy Sunday*

The dogma of the infallibility of the Bible is no more self-evident than in the infallibility of the Pope.

—*Thomas Henry Huxley*

Nobody ever outgrows scripture; the book widens and deepens with our years.

—*Charles Spurgeon*

See AFTERLIFE, CHRISTIANITY, GOD, HELL

Bigotry

There are only two ways to be unprejudiced and impartial. One is to be completely ignorant. The other is to be completely indifferent. Bias and prejudice are attitudes to be kept in hand, not attitudes to be avoided.

—*Charles Curtis*

If we believe absurdities, we shall commit atrocities.

—*Voltaire*

The mind of a bigot is like the pupil of an eye; the more light you pour into it, the more it will contract.

—*Oliver Wendell Holmes*

All looks yellow to a jaundiced eye.

—*Alexander Pope*

Prejudice not founded on reason cannot be removed by argument.

—*Samuel Johnson*

Prejudice is the child of ignorance.

—*William Hazlitt*

Prejudice is an opinion without judgment.

—Voltaire

Nothing is so firmly believed as what is least known.

—Michel de Montaigne

One may no more live in the world without picking up the moral prejudices of the world, than one would be able to go to hell without perspiring.

—H. L. Mencken

See **PREJUDICE**

Blacks

To like an individual because he's black is just as insulting as to dislike him because he isn't white.

—E. Cumming

The American nation ought to be ashamed of themselves for letting their medals be won by Negroes.

—Adolf Hitler

A racially integrated community is a chronological term timed from the entrance of the first black family to the exit of the last white family.

—Saul Alinsky

I want to be the white man's brother, not his brother-in-law.

—Martin Luther King, Jr.

You can't hold a man down without staying down with him.

—Booker T. Washington

The man ain't prejudiced. He doesn't care what color his slaves are.

—C. Anderson

Some people have a wonderful way of looking at things. Like the ones who hire us to babysit so they can go to a Ku Klux Klan meeting.

—Dick Gregory

I believe in white supremacy until the blacks are educated to a point of responsibility.

—John Wayne

Blame

To show resentment at a reproach is to acknowledge that one may have deserved it.

—*Tacitus*

Those see nothing but faults that seek for nothing else.

—*Thomas Fuller*

If we had no faults of our own we would not take so much pleasure in noticing those of others.

—*François de La Rochefoucauld*

The dead are indifferent to slander, but the living can die of it.

—*Voltaire*

There is luxury in self-reproach. When we blame ourselves, we feel no one else has a right to blame us.

—*Oscar Wilde*

People say ill-natured things without design, but not without having a pleasure in it.

—*William Hazlitt*

If you hear that someone is speaking ill of you, instead of trying to defend yourself, you should say: "He obviously does not know me very well, since there are so many other faults he could have mentioned."

—Epictetus

Blindness

I can see, and that is why I can be so happy in what you call the dark, but which to me is golden. I can see a God-made world, not a man-made world.

—Helen Keller

You are blind, and I am deaf and dumb, so let us touch hands and understand.

—Kahlil Gibran

If thou art a master, be sometimes blind, if a servant, sometimes deaf.

—Thomas Fuller

Be willing to have it so. Acceptance of what has happened is the first step to overcoming the consequences of any misfortune.

—William James

Never bend your head. Always hold it high. Look the world straight in the face.

—Helen Keller

There's none so blind as they that won't see.

—Jonathan Swift

Blushing

Man is the only animal that blushes. Or needs to.

—Mark Twain

The man that blushes is not quite a brute.

—Edward Young

Innocence is not accustomed to blush.

—Molière

Men blush less for their crimes than for their weaknesses and vanity.

—Jean de La Bruyère

The blush is beautiful, but it is sometimes inconvenient.

—*Carlo Goldoni*

See EMOTION

Body

The body is a thing. The soul is also a thing. Man is not a thing, but a drama.

—*O. Gassert*

One's eyes are what one is, one's mouth what one becomes.

—*John Galsworthy*

Grace is to the body what clear thinking is to the mind.

—*François de La Rochefoucald*

We speak with our lips to explain, with our throats to convince.

—*Chazal*

When one shuts one eye, one does not hear everything.

—Anon.

The eyes and ears are bad mistresses for men, if they have barbarous souls.

—Heraclitus

The head sublime, the heart pathos, the genitals beauty, hands and feet proportion.

—William Blake

See HEALTH

Books

There are two kinds of books, those that no one reads and those that no one ought to read.

—H. L. Mencken

I suggest that the only books that influence us are those for which we are ready and which have gone a little farther down our particular path than we have gone ourselves.

—C. S. Forester

A book is like a garden carried in the pocket.

—Anon.

We live in an age that reads too much to be wise.

—Oscar Wilde

The most beautiful things are those that madness prompts and reason writes.

—André Gide

A true poet does not bother to be poetical. Nor does a nursery gardener scent his roses.

—Jean Cocteau

Literature is a luxury. Fiction is a necessity.

—G. K. Chesterton

Real books should be the offspring not of daylight and casual talk but of darkness and silence.

—Marcel Proust

A book is a mirror; if an ass peers into it you can't expect an apostle to peer out.

—George Christoph Lichtenberg

A man may as well expect to grow stronger by always eating as wiser by always reading.

—David Collier

There is more treasure in books than in all the pirate's loot on Treasure Island, and best of all, you can enjoy these riches every day of your life.

—*Walt Disney*

How vain it is to sit down to write when you have not stood up to live.

—*Henry David Thoreau*

Never lend books, for no one ever returns them. The only books I have in my library are those that other folk have lent me.

—*Anatole France*

Everything one records contains a grain of hope, no matter how deeply it may come from despair.

—*Elias Canetti*

Neither Christ nor Buddha nor Socrates wrote a book, for to do that is to exchange life for a logical process.

—*William Butler Yeats*

Books are not men, and yet they are alive.

—*Stephen Vincent Benét*

A best seller was a book which somehow sold well simply because it was selling well.

—*S. Boorstein*

Some books seem to have been written not to teach us anything but to let us know that the author has known something.

—Johann Wolfgang von Goethe

There is hardly any grief that an hour's reading will not dissipate.

—Baron de Montesquieu

A room without books is a body without soul.

—Cicero

Solomon made a book of proverbs, but a book of proverbs never made a Solomon.

—Anon.

Every work of art adheres to some system of morality. But if it be really a work of art, it must contain the essential criticism of the morality to which it adheres.

—D. H. Lawrence

One of the marks of a great poet is that he creates his own family of words and teaches them to live together in harmony and to help one another.

—Gerald Brenan

The road to ignorance is paved with good editors.

—George Bernard Shaw

No book is really worth reading at the age of ten which is not equally, and often far more, worth reading at the age of fifty and beyond.

—*C. S. Lewis*

If we encounter a man of rare intellect we should ask him what books he reads.

—*Ralph Waldo Emerson*

When I am dead, I hope it may be said:
"His sins were scarlet, but his books were read."

—*Hilaire Belloc*

Some books are undeservedly forgotten; none are undeservedly remembered.

—*W. H. Auden*

Manuscript: something submitted in haste and returned at leisure.

—*Lewis Carroll*

To expect a man to retain everything that he has ever read is like expecting him to carry about in his body everything he has ever eaten.

—*Arthur Schopenhauer*

A classic is something that everyone wants to have read and nobody wants to read.

—*Mark Twain*

I would never read a book if it were possible for me to talk half an hour with the man who wrote it.

—*Woodrow Wilson*

See AUTHORS, EDUCATION, LEARNING, LITERATURE, WORDS

Boredom

It is a sad truth that everyone is a bore to someone.

—*L. Miller*

Dullness is decent in the church and state.

—*John Dryden*

One can be bored until boredom becomes a mystical experience.

—*Logan Pearsall Smith*

In heaven, they will bore you; in hell, you will bore them.

—*K. Whitehorn*

Risk is what separates the good part of life from the tedium.

—*J. Zero*

Society is now one polished horde,
Formed of two mighty tribes, the Bores and Bored.

—*Lord Byron*

Boredom is the most horrible of wolves.

—*John Giono*

The great advantage of being in a rut is that when one is in a rut, one knows exactly where one is.

—*Arnold Bennett*

Punctuality is the virtue of the bored.

—*Evelyn Waugh*

I sometimes say to myself: "Life is too short to be worth troubling about." Yet if a bore calls on me, prevents me from going out or attending to my affairs, I lose patience and cannot endure it for half an hour.

—*Marquis de Vauvenargues*

Boredom is one face of death.

—J. Green

Bravery

Many would be coward if they had courage enough.

—Thomas Fuller

Patience and fortitude conquer all things.

—Ralph Waldo Emerson

The powers of the soul are commensurate with its needs.

—Ralph Waldo Emerson

It's not life that counts but the fortitude you bring into it.

—John Galsworthy

Perfect courage means doing unwitnessed what we would be capable of with the world looking on.

—François de La Rochefoucauld

I am the master of my fate;
I am the captain of my soul.

—William Ernest Henley

Keep your fears to yourself, but share your courage with others.

—*Robert Louis Stevenson*

For those who will fight bravely and not yield, there is triumphant victory over all the dark things of life.

—*J. Allen*

Whistling to keep up courage is good practice for whistling.

—*Henry Hoskins*

Business

America can no more survive and grow without big business than it can survive and grow without small business.

—*Benjamin Franklin*

There is hardly anything in the world that some man cannot make a little worse and sell a little cheaper.

—*John Ruskin*

There are very honest people who do not think they have had a bargain unless they have cheated a merchant.

—Anatole France

One third of the people in the U.S. promote while the other two thirds provide.

—Will Rogers

The chief business of the American people is business.

—Calvin Coolidge

A corporation cannot blush.

—H. Walsh

Whatever is not nailed down is mine. Whatever I can pry loose is not nailed down.

—Collis P. Huntington

Junk is the ultimate merchandise. The junk merchant does not sell his product to the consumer; he sells the consumer to the product. He does not improve and simplify his merchandise; he degrades and simplifies the client.

—John Burroughs

See TAXES

Candor

All truths that are kept silent become poison.

—Friedrich Wilhelm Nietzsche

Truth is such a rare thing, it is delightful to tell it.

—Emily Dickinson

When in doubt, tell the truth.

—Mark Twain

A man had rather have a hundred lies told of him than one truth which he does not wish should be told.

—Samuel Johnson

A writer is congenitally unable to tell the truth, and that is why we call what he writes fiction.

—William Faulkner

You have to remember: the truth is funny.

—Timothy Leary

Sometimes we have to change the truth in order to remember it.

—George Santayana

Uninterpreted truth is as useless as buried gold.

—Lytton Strachey

See ADVICE, CRITICISM

Cats

When I play with my cat, who knows but that she regards me more as a plaything than I do her.

—Michel de Montaigne

No matter how much cats fight, there always seem to be plenty of kittens.

—Abraham Lincoln

Those who'll play with cats must expect to be scratched.

—Miguel de Cervantes

See ANIMALS, DOGS

Celebrity

Censure is the tax a man pays to the public for being eminent.

—Jonathan Swift

The great are great only because we are on our knees.

—Pierre de Proudhon

If fame is to come only after death, I am in no hurry for it.

—Martial

Greatness lies not in being strong, but in the right use of strength.

—Henry Ward Beecher

A celebrity is a person who works hard all his life to become well known, then wears dark glasses to avoid being recognized.

—Fred Allen

Celebrity sells dearly what we think she gives.

—Souvestre

See FAME

Change

Change is not progress.

—*H. L. Mencken*

Civilization is a movement and not a condition. A voyage and not a harbor.

—*Arnold Toynbee*

If you want to make enemies, try to change something.

—*Woodrow Wilson*

It's hard for me to get used to these changing times, I can remember when the air was clean and sex was dirty.

—*George Burns*

Things don't change, but, by and by, our wishes change.

—*Marcel Proust*

Nothing endures but change.

—*Heraclitus*

You can not step twice into the same river, for other waters are continually flowing on.

—*Heraclitus*

Not everything that is faced can be changed, but nothing can be changed until it is faced.

—James Baldwin

The reasonable man adapts himself to the world; the unreasonable one persists in trying to adapt the world to himself. Therefore, all progress depends on the unreasonable man.

—George Bernard Shaw

Character

If a man does not keep pace with his companions, perhaps it is because he hears a different drummer. Let him step to the music which he hears, however measured or far away.

—Henry David Thoreau

Separate we come, and separate we go, and this be it known, is all that we know.

—Conrad Aiken

In order to be irreplaceable, one must always be different.

—Coco Chanel

When you look into a mirror, you do not see your reflection; your reflection sees you.

—Daedalus

Nothing really sets human nature free but self control.

—Paul Bottome

Everyone is necessarily the hero of his own life story.

—John Barth

It is better to be hated for what you are than loved for what you are not.

—André Gide

Blessed is he who has reached the point of no return and knows it, for he shall enjoy living.

—William Bennett

Better keep yourself clean and bright; you are the window through which you must see the world.

—George Bernard Shaw

When a man's fight begins within himself, he is worth something.

—Robert Browning

Do not say things. What you are stands over you the while, and thunders so that I cannot hear what you say to the contrary.

—Ralph Waldo Emerson

The most important thing is to be whatever you are without shame.

—*Rod Steiger*

Until we lose ourselves, there is no hope of finding ourselves.

—*Henry Miller*

The universe seems bankrupt as soon as we begin to discuss the character of individuals.

—*Henry David Thoreau*

All that we are is the result of what we have thought. The mind is everything. What we think, we become.

—*Buddha*

Acquit me, or do not acquit me, but be sure that I shall not alter my way of life, no, not if I have to die for it many times.

—*Socrates*

Character builds slowly, but it can be torn down again with incredible swiftness.

—*Faith Baldwin*

When you make a world tolerable for yourself, you make a world tolerable for others.

—*Anaïs Nin*

See CONVICTIONS

Charm

The greatest mistake is trying to be more agreeable than you can be.

—*Walter Bagehot*

Nothing is so old as a dilapidated charm.

—*Emily Dickinson*

If you have it [charm], you don't need to have anything else, and if you don't have it, it doesn't much matter what else you have.

—*James M. Barrie*

Chastity

Chastity: the most unnatural of sexual perversions.

—*Aldous Huxley*

Virtue by calculation is the virtue of vice.

—*Joseph Joubert*

Marriage has many pains, but celibacy has no pleasures.

—*Samuel Johnson*

Give me chastity and continency, but not yet.

—*St. Augustine*

The resistance of a woman is not always proof of her virtue, but more frequently of her experience.

—*Ninon de L'Enclos*

Of all sexual aberrations, perhaps the most peculiar is chastity.

—*Remy de Gourmont*

An unattempted woman can not boast of her chastity.

—*Michel de Montaigne*

Children

Posterity is the patriotic name for grandchildren.

—*Art Linkletter*

Every child is born a genius.

—*Robert Fuller*

We can't form our children on our own concepts; we must take them and love them as God gives them to us.

—*Johann Wolfgang von Goethe*

Something you consider bad may bring out your child's talents; something you consider good may stifle them.

—*François René de Chateaubriand*

We find delight in the beauty and happiness of children that makes the heart too big for the body.

—*Ralph Waldo Emerson*

Children begin by loving their parents; as they grow older they judge them; sometimes they forgive them.

—*Oscar Wilde*

The thorns which I have reaped are of the tree I planted.

—*Lord Byron*

The more you love your children, the more care you should take to neglect them occasionally. The web of affection can be drawn too tight.

—*D. Sutton*

The young man knows the rules, but the old man knows the exceptions.

—*Oliver Wendell Holmes*

Children are a great comfort in your old age and they help you to reach it faster, too.

—*Lionel Kaufman*

The maturity of man: to have reacquired the seriousness he had as a child at play.

—*Friedrich Wilhelm Nietzsche*

Before I got married, I had six theories about bringing up children; now I have six children and no theories.

—*Lord Rochester*

How sharper than a serpent's tooth it is
To have a thankless child.

—*William Shakespeare:King Lear*

The best way to keep children at home is to make the atmosphere pleasant and let the air out of the tires.

—Dorothy Parker

Allow children to be happy in their own way, for what better way will they ever find?

—Samuel Johnson

All God's children are not beautiful; most of God's children are, in fact, barely presentable.

—Fran Lebowitz

I love children, especially when they cry. Then someone takes them away.

—Nancy Mitford

Adults are obsolete children

—Dr. Seuss

The fundamental defect of fathers is that they want their children to be a credit to them.

—Bertrand Russell

Our children will hate us too, y' know.

—Jack Lemmon

The mother of the year should be a sterilized woman with two children.

—*Paul Ehrlich*

Every boy in his heart would rather steal second base than an automobile.

—*Tom Clarke*

What is an adult? A child blown up by age.

—*Simone de Beauvoir*

Children sweeten labors, but they make misfortune more bitter.

—*Anon.*

Permissiveness is the principle of treating children as if they were adults and the tactic of making sure they never reach that stage.

—*Thomas Szasz*

My object will be, if possible, to form Christian men, for Christian boys I can scarcely hope to make.

—*Thurman Arnold*

See ADOLESCENCE, AGE, YOUTH

You don't have to be perfect to be Christ. All you have to do is stick your neck out and say the system sucks. They'll find a way of nailing you to the cross.

—Eric Burdon

If Jesus Christ were to come today, people would not even crucify him. They would ask him to dinner and hear what he had to say and make fun of it.

—Thomas Carlyle

Christians never were meant to be respectable.

—Harry Emerson Fosdick

The good news is that Jesus is coming back. The bad news is that He's really pissed off.

—Bob Hope

Christianity is completed Judaism, or it is nothing.

—Benjamin Disraeli

If Christian nations were nations of Christians, there would be no wars.

—Soame Jenyns

Christendom has done away with Christianity without being quite aware of it.

—*Sören Kierkegaard*

No kingdom has ever had as many civil wars as the kingdom of Christ.

—*Baron de Montesquieu*

To the frivolous, Christianity is certainly not glad tidings, for it wishes first of all to make them serious.

—*Sören Kierkegaard*

Christianity is so full of fraud, that any honest man should renounce the whole shebang and espouse atheism instead.

—*Paul Blanchard*

See AFTERLIFE, BIBLE, GOD

Civilization

We live in a Newtonian world of Einsteinian physics ruled by Frankensteinian logic.

—*Bertrand Russell*

Civilization is, after all, but a coat of paint that washes away when the rain falls.

—Auguste Rodin

Perfection of means and confusion of ends seem to characterize our age.

—Albert Einstein

Civilization has spread until television and jet bombers can be heard everywhere.

—Herbert Prochnow

Civilization is progress from an indefinite incoherent homogeneity toward a definite coherent heterogeneity.

—Herbert Spencer

Human history becomes more and more a race between education and catastrophe.

—H. G. Wells

See MAN

Committees

A camel looks like a horse that was planned by a committee.

—Vogue Magazine

Nothing is every accomplished by a committee unless it consists of three members, one of whom happens to be sick and the other absent.

—Hendrik Williem Van Loon

A committee is a thing which takes a week to do what one good man can do in an hour.

—Elbert Hubbard

Committee: a group of men who keep minutes and waste hours.

—Anon.

Committee: a group of the unfit appointed by the unwilling to do the unnecessary.

—Stewart Harrol

To kill time, a committee meeting is the perfect weapon.

—Fred Allen

Conceit

Conceit is incompatible with understanding.

—*Leo Tolstoy*

When a man is wrapped up in himself, he makes a pretty small package.

—*John Ruskin*

He was like a cock who thought the sun had risen to hear him crow.

—*George Eliot*

Conceit is God's gift to little men.

—*Bruce Barton*

See EGO

Confidence

Confidence: the feeling that makes one believe a man, even when one knows that one would lie in his place.

—*H. L. Mencken*

Confidence is simply the fervent assured feeling you have before you fall flat on your face.

—C. Bruder

All you need in this life is ignorance and confidence and then success is sure.

—Mark Twain

You have noticed that the less I known about a subject, the more confidence I have, and the more light I throw on it.

—Mark Twain

See ACTION, SUCCESS

Conformity

There is no conversation more boring than where everybody agrees.

—Michel de Montaigne

Comedy is the last refuge of the non-conformist mind.

—George Seldes

Force, violence, pressure, or compulsion with a view to conformity are both uncivilized and undemocratic.

—Mahatma Gandhi

Lots of times, you have to pretend to join a parade in which you are really not interested in order to get where you are going.

—Christopher Morley

Every society honors its live conformists and its dead trouble makers.

—M. McLaughlin

Conscience

Conscience is a cur that will let you get past it but that you cannot keep from barking.

—Anon.

Men of character are the conscience of the society to which they belong.

—Ralph Waldo Emerson

Conscience is the inner voice that warns us somebody may be looking.

—*H. L. Mencken*

Conscience and cowardice are really the same things.

—*Oscar Wilde*

Conservative

A conservative is a man who just sits and thinks, mostly sits.

—*Woodrow Wilson*

A conservative is a man with two perfectly good legs who has never learned to walk.

—*Franklin D. Roosevelt*

Men are conservatives when they are least vigorous, or when they are most luxurious. They are conservatives after dinner.

—*Ralph Waldo Emerson*

Conservative: a statesman who is enamored of existing evils, as distinguished from the Liberal who wishes to replace them with others.

—*Ambrose Bierce*

Loyalty to petrified opinion never yet broke a chain or freed a human soul.

—Mark Twain

No man can be a conservative until he has something to lose.

—J. Warburg

Men who are orthodox when they are young are in danger of being middle aged all their lives.

—Walter Lippman

See LIBERAL

Contentment

To me, old age is always fifteen years older than I am.

—Bernard Baruch

Winter is in my head, but spring is in my heart.

—Victor Hugo

He is a wise man who does not grieve for the things which he has not, but rejoices for those which he has.

—Epictetus

Before we set our hearts too much upon anything, let us examine how happy they are who already possess it.

—*François de La Rochefoucauld*

If wrinkles must be written upon our brows, let them not be written upon the heart. The spirit should not grow old.

—*James Garfield*

See **PEACE**

Conversation

I often quote myself: it adds spice to my conversation.

—*George Bernard Shaw*

A good listener is not only popular everywhere, but after a while, he knows something.

—*Wilson Mizner*

Better to remain silent and to be thought a fool than to speak out and remove all doubt.

—*Abraham Lincoln*

Whenever one has anything unpleasant to say, one should always be quite candid.

—Oscar Wilde

He has occasional flashes of silence that make his conversation perfectly delightful.

—Sydney Smith

Wise men talk because they have something to say; fools, because they have to say something.

—Plato

Arguments are to be avoided; they are always vulgar and often convincing.

—Oscar Wilde

There are things which it is not only impossible to discuss intelligently, but which it is not even intelligent to discuss.

—Feodor Dostoevsky

See TALK

Convictions

A very popular error—having the courage of one's convictions; rather, it is a matter of having the courage for an attack upon one's convictions.

—Friedrich Wilhelm Nietzsche

So long as I am acting from duty and conviction, I am indifferent to taunts and jeers; I think they will probably do me more good than harm.

—Winston Churchill

Christians have burnt each other quite persuaded that all the apostles would have done as they did.

—Lory Byron

Strong beliefs win strong men, and then make them stronger.

—Walter Bagehot

Neutral men are the devil's allies.

—E. Chapin

One needs to be slow to form convictions, but once formed, they must be defended against the heaviest odds.

—*Mahatma Gandhi*

See BELIEVING

Creativity

All men are creative, but few are artists.

—*Paul Goodman*

To a writer or painter, creation is the repayment of a debt. He suffers from a perpetual bad conscience until he has done this.

—*Gerald Brenan*

The creative impulses of man are always at war with the possessive impulses.

—*Van Wyck Brooks*

A creator needs only one enthusiast to justify him.

—*Man Ray*

There is nothing mysterious about originality, nothing fantastic. Originality is merely the step beyond.

—L. Danze

You've got to create a dream. You've got to uphold the dream. If you can't, then bugger it. Go back to the factory, or go back to the desk.

—Eric Burdon

Some men see things as they are and say why. I dream things that never were and say, "Why not?"

—John F. Kennedy

Creativity can solve almost any problem. The creative act, the defeat of habit by originality overcomes everything.

—George Lois

See ART, MUSIC, WORDS

Crime

Every once in a while, some feller without a single bad habit gets caught.

—Kin Hubbard

A criminal is a person with predatory instincts who has not sufficient capital to form a corporation.

—Howard Scott

Most people fancy themselves innocent of those crimes of which they can not be convicted.

—Seneca

If England treats her criminals the way she has treated me, she doesn't deserve to have any.

—Oscar Wilde

Many commit the same crime with very different results. One bears a cross for his crime, the other a crown.

—Bertrand de Juvenal

When I see the ten most wanted list, I always have this thought, if we'd made them feel wanted earlier, they wouldn't be wanted now.

—Eddie Cantor

Capital punishment is as fundamentally wrong as a cure for crime as charity is wrong as a cure for poverty.

—Henry Ford

It is worse than a crime; it is a blunder.

—Joseph Fouché

See EVIL, LAW

Criticism

Show me a man who insists that he welcomes criticism if only it is constructive, and I will show you a man who does not want any criticism at all.

—Harold L. Ickes

They couldn't find the artist, so they hung the picture.

—Anon.

The covers of this book are too far apart.

—Ambrose Bierce

There is no man so friendless but that he can find a friend sincere enough to tell him disagreeable truths.

—Edward Bulwer-Lytton

It was one of those plays in which the actors, unfortunately, enunciated very clearly.

—Robert Benchley

See CANDOR, ADVICE

Death keeps no calendar.

—*Thomas Fuller*

One may live as a conqueror, a king, or a magistrate, but he must die as a man.

—*Daniel Webster*

But my troth, I care not, a man can die but once. We owe God a death.

—*William Shakespeare*

You can't tell how good it is to be alive till you're facing death because you don't live till then.

—*John Galsworthy*

It is good to die before one has done anything deserving death.

—*Anaxandrides*

Some men are more missed than lamented, when they die. Others are deeply mourned but scarcely missed.

—*François de La Rochefoucauld*

Nothing is truer in a sense than a funeral oration. It tells precisely what the dead man should have been.

—*J. Vaperean*

To die will be an awfully big adventure.

—*James M. Barrie*

We sometimes congratulate ourselves at the moment of waking from a troubled dream; it may be so the moment after death.

—*Nathaniel Hawthorne*

After your death you will be what you were before your birth.

—*Arthur Schopenhauer*

The most frightful idea that has ever corroded human nature—the idea of eternal punishment.

—*John Morley*

All I desire for my own funeral is not to be buried alive.

—*G. K. Chesterton*

If death did not exist, it would be necessary to invent it.

—*J. Milhaud*

There's one thing that keeps surprising you about stormy old friends after they die—their silence.

—*Ben Hecht*

A man's dying is more the survivors' affair than his own.

—*Thomas Mann*

I am going to seek a grand perhaps...

—*François Rabelais*

It matters not how a man dies, but how he lives.

—*Samuel Johnson*

Until death, it is all life.

—*Miguel de Cervantes*

Every day is a little life; every waking and rising a little birth, every fresh morning a little youth, every going to rest and sleep a little death.

—*Arthur Schopenhauer*

I am dying beyond my means.

—*Oscar Wilde*

Into the darkness they go, the wise and the lovely.

—*Edna St. Vincent Millay*

It is not death that alarms me, but dying.

—Michel de Montaigna

The good man should go on living as long as he ought to, not just as long as he likes.

—Seneca

We must laugh before we are happy, for fear we die before we laugh at all.

—Jean de La Bruyere

To die is easy when we are in perfect health. On a fine spring morning, out of doors, mind and body sound and exhilarated, it would be nothing to lie down on the turf and pass away.

—Mark Rutherford

It's not that I'm afraid to die. I just don't want to be there when it happens.

—Woody Allen

To save a man's life against his will is the same as killing him.

—Horace

If some persons died, and others did not die, death would indeed be a terrible affliction.

—Jean de La Bruyere

If a man hasn't discovered something that he will die for, he isn't fit to live.

—*Martin Luther King, Jr.*

Our repugnance to death increases in proportion to our consciousness of having lived in vain.

—*William Hazlitt*

To the psychiatrist an old man who cannot bid farewell to life appears as feeble and sickly as a young man who is unable to embrace it.

—*Carl Jung*

No man should be afraid to die who hath understood what it is to live.

—*Thomas Fuller*

While I thought that I was learning how to live, I have been learning how to die.

—*Leonardo da Vinci*

Moderate lamentation is the right of the dead, excessive grief the enemy to the living.

—*William Shakespeare: All's Well That Ends Well*

Worldly faces never look so worldly as at a funeral.

—*T. S. Eliot*

See AFTERLIFE, LIFE

Debt

Debt is the fatal disease of republics, the first thing and the mightiest to undermine governments and corrupt the people.

—Wendell Phillips

Pride does not wish to owe and vanity does not wish to pay.

—François de La Rochefoucauld

Blessed are the young for they shall inherit the national debt.

—Herbert Hoover

Never run into debt, not if you can find anything else to run into.

—Josh Billings

Some people use one half their ingenuity to get into debt, and the other half to avoid paying it.

—George Prentice

We can only pay our debt to the past by putting the future in debt to ourselves.

—John Buchan

See **MONEY**

Deception

You may be deceived if you trust too much, but you will live in torment if you do not trust enough.

—Frank Crane

We are never deceived. We deceive ourselves.

—Johann Wolfgang von Goethe

Deceive not thy physician, confessor, nor lawyer.

—George Herbert

It is a double pleasure to deceive the deceiver.

—Jean de La Fontaine

It is true that you may fool all the people some of the time; you can even fool some of the people all the time; but you cannot fool all of the people all the time.

—Abraham Lincoln

The ring always believes that the finger lives for it.

—Chazal

It is in the ability to deceive oneself that the greatest talent is shown.

—Anatole France

See LYING

Definitions

It is almost impossible to state what one in fact believes because it is almost impossible to hold a belief and to define it at the same time.

—William Carlos Williams

A definition is the enclosing of a wilderness of ideas within a wall of words.

—Samuel Butler

I had rather feel compunction than understand the meaning of it.

—Thomas à Kempis

Democracy

In Switzerland, they had brotherly love, five hundred years of democracy, and peace, and what did they produce: the cuckoo clock.

—Orson Welles

Democracy is the art of running the circus from the monkey cage.

—H. L. Mencken

I believe in democracy because it releases the energies of every human being.

—Woodrow Wilson

Democracy means government by discussion, but it is only effective if you can stop people talking.

—Clement Atlee

Democracy gives every man the right to be his own oppressor.

—John Lowell

Democracy substitutes election by the incompetent many for appointment by the corrupt few.

—*George Bernard Shaw*

Democracy means simply the bludgeoning of the people by the people for the people.

—*Oscar Wilde*

The job of a citizen is to keep his mouth open.

—*Günther Grass*

Democracy consists of choosing your dictators after they've told you what you think it is you want to hear.

—*Arnold Coven*

Democracy is based upon the conviction that there are extraordinary possibilities in ordinary people.

—*Harry Emerson Fosdick*

The ship of democracy which has weathered any storms may sink through the mutiny of those aboard.

—*Grover Cleveland*

It's not the voting that's democracy; it's the counting.

—*Tom Stoppard*

See GOVERNMENT

Deprecation

Don't abuse your friends and expect them to consider it criticism.

—*E. W. Howe*

They condemn what they do not understand.

—*Cicero*

We would rather speak ill of ourselves than not talk of ourselves at all.

—*François de La Rochefoucauld*

Those who have free seats at a play hiss first.

—*Anon.*

See BLAME

Desire and Longing

The animal needing something knows how much it needs; the man does not.

—*Democritus of Abdera*

Life contains but two tragedies. One is not to get your heart's desire; the other is to get it.

—*Socrates*

Every seed is a longing.

—*Kahlil Gibran*

The average man who does not know what to do with his life wants another one which will last forever.

—*Anatole France*

It is for the superfluous we sweat.

—*Seneca*

He who desires, but acts not, breeds pestilence.

—*William Blake*

Desire is half of life; indifference is half of death.

—*Kahlil Gibran*

Much will have more.

—Ralph Waldo Emerson

An aspiration is a joy forever, a possession as solid as a landed estate.

—Adlai Stevenson

We grow weary of those things (and perhaps soonest) which we most desire.

—Samuel Butler

Desperation

When we are flat on our back, there is no way to look but up.

—Roger Babson

Despair is the damp of hell as joy is the serenity of heaven.

—John Donne

Facing it, always facing it, that's the way to get through. Face it.

—Joseph Conrad

Walk on, walk on, with hope in your heart; and you'll never walk alone; you'll never walk alone.

—*Rodgers & Hammerstein*

I must lose myself in action lest I wither in despair.

—*Alfred Lord Tennyson*

Never despair. But if you do, work on in despair.

—*D. Burke*

When a man has reached a condition in which he believes that a thing must happen because he does not wish it, and that what he wishes to happen can never be, this is really the state called despair.

—*Arthur Schopenhauer*

See ALCOHOL, EMPTINESS

Diet

Tell me what you eat, and I'll tell you what you are.

—*Anthelme Brillat-Savarin*

He dreamed he was eating shredded wheat and woke up to find the mattress half gone.

—*Fred Allen*

As a child, my family's meal consisted of two choices: take it or leave it.

—*Buddy Hackett*

I told my doctor I got very tired when I go on a diet, so he gave me pep pills. Know what happened? I ate faster.

—*Joe E. Lewis*

The chief excitement in a woman's life is spotting women who are fatter than she is.

—*Helen Rowland*

See FOOD, HEALTH

Diplomats

A diplomat is a man who always remembers a woman's birthday but never remembers her age.

—*Robert Frost*

A diplomat is one who can cut his neighbor's throat without his neighbor noticing it.

—Carlos P. Romulo

An appeaser is one who feeds a crocodile hoping it will eat him last.

—Winston Churchill

Diplomacy is the art of letting someone have your way.

—Daniele Vare

I have discovered the art of fooling diplomats. I speak the truth, and they never believe me.

—O. Di Cavour

See GOVERNMENT

Direction

The person who makes a success of living is the one who sees his goal steadily and aims for it unswervingly. That is dedication.

—Cecil B. De Mille

If you cry, "Forward," you must be sure to make clear the direction in which to go. Don't you see that if you fail to do that and simply call out the word to a monk and a revolutionary, they will go in precisely opposite directions.

—*Anton Chekhov*

The dodo flies backward because he doesn't care to see where he's going, but wants to see where he's been.

—*Fred Allen*

Disappointment

The disappointment of manhood succeeds the delusion of youth.

—*Benjamin Disraeli*

For of all sad words of tongue or pen,
The saddest are these: "It might have been!"

—*John Greenleaf Whittier*

How disappointment tracks the steps of hope.

—*L. London*

Blessed be he who expects nothing, for he shall never be disappointed.

—*Jonathan Swift*

We mount to heaven mostly on the ruins of our cherished schemes, finding our failures were successes.

—*Bronson Alcott*

Disease

I wonder why ye can always read a doctor's bill an ye niver can read his purscription,

—*Finley Peter Dunne*

It takes a wise doctor to know when not to prescribe.

—*Baltasar Gracián*

Cure the disease and kill the patient.

—*Isaac*

How sickness enlarges the dimensions of man's self to himself.

—*Charles Lamb*

Formerly, when religion was strong and science weak, men mistook magic for medicine; now, when science is strong and religion weak, men mistake medicine for magic.

—*Thomas Szasz*

Optimistic lies have such immense therapeutic value that a doctor who cannot tell them convincingly has mistaken his profession.

—*George Bernard Shaw*

See DOCTORS, HEALTH

Dispute

Thrusting my nose firmly between his teeth, I threw him heavily to the ground on top of me.

—*Mark Twain*

Before you contradict an old man, my fair friend, you should endeavor to understand him.

—*George Santayana*

If you go in for argument, take care of your temper.
Your logic, if you have any, will take care of itself.

—Joseph Farrell

Discussion is an exchange of knowledge, argument an
exchange of ignorance.

—Robert Quillen

I dislike arguments, of any kind. They are always vulgar
and often convincing.

—Oscar Wilde

There is no arguing with Johnson: for if his pistol misses
fire, he knocks you down with the butt end of it.

—Oliver Goldsmith

If you can't answer a man's arguments, all is not lost;
you can still call him vile names.

—Elbert Hubbard

Silence is one of the hardest things to refute.

—Josh Billings

I never make the mistake of arguing with people for
whose opinions I have no respect.

—Edward Gibbon

It is labor in vain to dispute with a man unless somebody be in company to whose judgment you would both submit.

—Anon.

There is no more sense in having an argument with a man so stupid he doesn't know you have the better of him.

—John Roper

You raise your voice when you should reinforce your argument.

—Samuel Johnson

See ANGER

Divorce

Marriage is grounds for divorce.

—Anon.

Love the quest; marriage the conquest; divorce the inquest.

—Helen Rowland

The mind that renounces once and forever a futile hope has its compensation in ever-growing calm.

—*George Gissing*

How many a thing which we cast to the ground, when others pick it up becomes a gem.

—*George Meredith*

It's well to be off with the old woman before you're on with the new.

—*George Bernard Shaw*

See ALIMONY, MARRIAGE

Doctors

God heals, and the doctor takes the fee.

—*Benjamin Franklin*

The threat of a neglected cold is for doctors what the threat of purgatory is for priests: a gold mine.

—*Nicolas Chamfort*

It is astonishing with how little reading a doctor can practice medicine, but it is not astonishing how badly he may do it.

—William Osler

Whenever a doctor cannot do good, he must be kept from doing harm.

—Hippocrates

Doctors are men who prescribe medicines of which they know little to cure diseases of which they know less in human beings of whom they know nothing.

—Voltaire

See HEALTH

Dogs

A dog is the only thing on this earth that loves you more than he loves himself.

—Josh Billings

If you pick up a starving dog and make him prosperous, he will not bite you. That is the principal difference between a dog and a man.

—*Mark Twain*

A reasonable number of fleas is good for a dog, keeps him from brooding over being a dog.

—*Edward Westcott*

See ANIMALS, CATS

Drama

Not to go to the theater is like making one's toilet without a mirror.

—*Arthur Schopenhauer*

As long as more people will pay admission to a theater to see a naked body than to see a naked brain, the drama will languish.

—*George Bernard Shaw*

If you want something from an audience, you give blood to their fantasies. It's the ultimate hustle.

—*Marlon Brando*

One of my chief regrets during my years in the theater is that I couldn't sit in the audience and watch me.

—*John Barrymore*

The world is a comedy to those who think and a tragedy to those who feel.

—*Horace Walpole*

See ACTING, HOLLYWOOD, TELEVISION

Dreams

I am so unhappy at the present time that in my dreams I am indescribably happy.

—*Sören Kierkegaard*

If people would recount their dreams truthfully, one might divine character more correctly from dreams than from faces.

—*George Christoph Lichtenberg*

The inquiry into a dream is another dream.

—*Lord Halifax*

The republic is a dream,
Nothing happens unless first a dream.

—*Carl Sandburg*

What is beneath the earth is quite as natural as what is above ground, and he who cannot summon spirits in the daytime under the open sky will not evoke them at midnight in a vault.

—*Johann Wolfgang von Goethe*

See HOPE

Education

It is better to speak wisdom foolishly like the saints than to speak folly wisely like the deans.

—*G. K. Chesterton*

An education obtained with money is worse than no education obtained at all.

—*Socrates*

When a subject becomes totally obsolete, we make it a required course.

—Peter Drucker

A man who has never gone to school may steal from a freight car, but if he has had a university education, he may steal from the whole railroad.

—Theodore Roosevelt

If a man's education is finished, he is finished.

—Edward Filene

It now costs more to amuse a child than it once did to educate his father.

—Vaughan Monroe

What does not destroy me makes me stronger.

—Friedrich Wilhelm Nietzsche

It doesn't make much difference what you study so long as you don't like it.

—Finley Peter Dunne

In the first place, God made idiots. This was for practice. Then he made school boards.

—Mark Twain

Education is the ability to listen to almost anything without losing your temper or self-confidence.

—Anon.

Crafty men condemn studies; simple men admire them, and wise men use them.

—Francis Bacon

The eagle never lost so much time as when he submitted to learn of the crow.

—William Blake

An educated man may earn more, but it takes him about twenty years after graduating to get educated.

—Herbert Prochnow

Our American professors like their literature clear and cold and pure and very dead.

—Sinclair Lewis

A learned blockhead is a greater blockhead than an ignorant one.

—Benjamin Franklin

Soap and education are not as sudden as a massacre, but they are more deadly in the long run.

—Mark Twain

Stand firm in your refusal to remain conscious during algebra. In real life, I assure you there is no such thing as algebra.

—*Fran Lebowitz*

How is it possible to expect that mankind will take advice when they will not so much as take warning.

—*Jonathan Swift*

Nothing in education is so astonishing as the amount of ignorance it accumulates in the form of inert facts.

—*Henry Adams*

See BOOKS, LEARNING, WORDS

Ego

When a man is wrapped up in himself, he makes a pretty small package.

—*John Ruskin*

Every man is of importance to himself.

—*Samuel Johnson*

Never to talk about oneself is a very refined form of hypocrisy.

—*Friedrich Wilhelm Nietzsche*

There are two sides to every question: my side and the wrong side.

—*Oscar Levant*

To love oneself is the beginning of a life-long romance.

—*Oscar Wilde*

The golden fleece of self love is proof against cudgel blows but not against pin pricks.

—*Friedrich Wilhelm Nietzsche*

He that falls in love with himself will have no rivals.

—*Benjamin Franklin*

You have no idea of what a poor opinion I have of myself, and how little I deserve it.

—*William Gilbert*

See EMOTION

Emotion

Anger always thinks it has power beyond its power.

—Publilius Syrus

To be angry is to revenge the faults of others upon ourselves.

—Alexander Pope

One doesn't love a place the less for having suffered in it.

—Jane Austen

There is always something ridiculous about the emotions of people whom one has ceased to love.

—Oscar Wilde

Nothing is more injurious to the character and to the intellect than the suppression of generous emotion.

—John Joy Chapman

See ANGER, BLUSHING, EGO, ENVY, FEAR, FEELINGS, GRIEF, HAPPINESS, HATE, HOPE, JEALOUSY, LOVE, SORROW

Emptiness

Our greatest pretenses are built up not to hide the evil and the ugly in us, but our emptiness.

—*Eric Hoffer*

When my cup is empty, I resign myself to its emptiness, but when it is half full, I resent its half fullness.

—*Kahlil Gibran*

In the small hours when the acrid stench of existence rises like sewer gas from every thing created, the emptiness of life seems more terrible than its misery.

—*Cyril Connolly*

Treat people as if they were what they ought to be and you help them to become what they are capable of being.

—*Johann Wolfgang van Goethe*

By virtue of being born to humanity, every human being has a right to the development and fulfillment of his potentialities as a human being.

—*Ashley Montague*

There is no meaning to life except the meaning man gives his life by the unfolding of his powers.

—*Eric Fromm*

See ALCOHOL, DESPERATION

Enemies

A friend is one who has the same enemies you have.

—*Abraham Lincoln*

It is difficult to say who do you the most mischief: enemies with the worst intentions or friends with the best intentions.

—*Edward Bulwer-Lytton*

Speak well of your enemies, sir. You made them.

—*Oscar Wilde*

A man cannot be too careful in the choice of his enemies.

—*Oscar Wilde*

Scratch a lover, and find a foe.

—*Dorothy Parker*

To forgive our enemies their virtues, that is a greater miracle.

—Voltaire

We has met the enemy, and it is us.

—Walt Kelly (Pogo)

Instead of loving your enemies treat your friends a little better.

—E. W. Howe

If you have no enemies, you are apt to be in the same predicament in regard to friends.

—Elbert Hubbard

It is not necessary to have enemies if you go out of your way to make friends.

—F. Dane

You will be quite friendly with your enemy when you both die.

—Kahlil Gibran

See FRIENDSHIP

England

The English have better sense than any other nation, and they are fools.

—*Klemens Von Metternich*

The English instinctively admire any man who has no talent and is modest about it.

—*Jame Agee*

If you want to eat well in England, eat three breakfasts.

—*W. Somerset Maugham*

An Englishman thinks he is moral when he is only uncomfortable.

—*George Bernard Shaw*

The British have a remarkable talent for keeping calm even when there is no crisis.

—*Franklin P. Jones*

Envy

The gilded sheath of pity conceals the dagger of envy.

—*Friedrich Wilhelm Nietzsche*

Oh what a bitter thing it is to look into happiness through another man's eyes.

—*William Shakespeare*

Few of us can stand prosperity, another man's, I mean.

—*Mark Twain*

Envy is more implacable than hatred.

—*François de La Rochefoucauld*

Man will do many things to get himself loved; he will do all things to get himself envied.

—*Mark Twain*

The dullard's envy of brilliant men is always assuaged by the suspicion that they will come to a bad end.

—*Max Beerbohm*

Envy, among other ingredients, has a mixture of love of justice in it. We are more angry at undeserved than at deserved good fortune.

—*William Hazlitt*

The silence of the envious is too noisy.

—*Kahlil Gibran*

Envy lurks at the bottom of the human heart like a viper in its hole.

—*Honoré de Balzac*

See EMOTION, JEALOUSY

Eternity

I can believe anything, but the justice of this world does not give me a very reassuring idea of the justice in the next. I am very much afraid that God will go on blundering; he will receive the wicked in paradise and hurl the good into hell.

—*Jules Renard*

Eternity is in love with the productions of time.

—*William Blake*

Nothing is eternal, alas, except eternity.

—Paul Fort

Do not the indiscretions which occur only after a person's life on earth is ended prove that nobody really believes in a future life?

—Marcel Proust

The fact of having been born is a bad augury for immortality.

—George Santayana

See AFTERLIFE, BIBLE, GOD

Evil

Man is almost always as wicked as his needs require.

—Giacomo Leopardi

You can not have power for good without having power for evil too.

—Anon.

Wicked people sometimes perform good actions. I suppose they wish to see if this gives as great a feeling of pleasure as the virtuous claim for it.

—*Nicolas Chamfort*

The wicked are always surprised to find that the good can be clever.

—*Marquis de Vauvenargues*

Money is the fruit of evil, as often as the root of it.

—*Henry Fielding*

Between two evils, I always pick the one I never tried before.

—*Mae West*

Even mother's milk nourishes murderers as well as heroes.

—*George Bernard Shaw*

Man is the only animal who causes pain to others with no other object than wanting to do so.

—*Arthur Schopenhauer*

Satan is inconsistent. He persuades a man not to go to synagogue on a cold morning; yet when the man does go, he follows him into it.

—*John Henry Cardinal Newman*

There are bad people who would be less dangerous if they had no good in them.

—*François de La Rochefoucauld*

I never wonder to see men wicked, but I often wonder to see them unashamed.

—*Jonathan Swift*

Bad men do what good men only dream.

—*Gavin Ewart*

The belief in a supernatural source of evil is not necessary; men alone are quite capable of every wickedness.

—*Joseph Conrad*

The Devil tempts men to be wicked that he may punish them for being so.

—*Samuel Butler*

Malicious men may die, but malice never.

—*Molière*

Few men are sufficiently discerning to appreciate the evil that they do.

—*François de La Rochefoucauld*

Bad nature never lacks an instructor.

—*Publilius Syrus*

Evil comes at leisure like the disease; good comes in a hurry like the doctor.

—*G. K. Chesterton*

A wonder is often expressed that the greatest criminals look like other men. The reason is that *they are like other men in many respects.*

—*William Hazlitt*

Many might go to heaven with half the labor they go to hell.

—*Samuel Johnson*

We have neither the strength nor the opportunity to accomplish all the good and all the evil which we design.

—*Marquis de Vauvenargues*

Grief and disappointment give rise to anger, anger to envy, envy to malice, and malice to grief again, till the whole circle be completed.

—*David Hume*

The Devil himself is good when he is pleased.

—*Thomas Fuller*

Kill a man, and you are a murderer. Kill millions of men, and you are a conquerer. Kill everyone, and you are a god.

—*Jean Rostand*

The lunatic's visions of horror are all drawn from the material of daily fact.

—*William James*

Cruelty isn't softened by tears; it feeds on them.

—*Publilius Syrus*

See CRIME, GOODWILL

Experience

Better a monosyllabic life than a ragged and muttered one; let its report be short and round like a rifle so that it may hear its own echo in the surrounding silence.

—*Henry David Thoreau*

Experience is not what happens to you. It is what you do with what happens to you.

—*Aldous Huxley*

Experience: a comb life gives you after you lose your hair.

—*Judith Stern*

Experience is the name men give to their follies or their sorrows.

—*Alfred De Musset*

One must pass through the circumference of time before arriving at the center of opportunity.

—*Baltasar Gracián*

Experience is a keen knife that hurts while it extracts the cataract that blinds.

—*Anon.*

Some people have had nothing else but experience.

—*Don Herolde*

Experiences are savings which a miser puts aside; wisdom is an inheritance which a wastrel can not exhaust.

—*Anon.*

Experience is simply the name we give our mistakes.

—*Oscar Wilde*

Technology . . . the knack of so arranging the world that we don't have to experience it.

—Max Frisch

Everyone is perfectly willing to learn from unpleasant experiences, if only the damage of the first lesson could be repaired.

—Georg Christoph Lichtenberg

Failure

We are all failures, at least the best of us.

—Anon.

You don't die in the U.S., you underachieve.

—Jerzy Kozinski

Failure has no friends.

—John F. Kennedy

A failure is a man who has blundered but who is not able to cash in the experience.

—Elbert Hubbard

He has spent all his life in letting down empty buckets into empty wells; and he is frittering away his age in trying to draw them up again.

—Sydney Smith

Nothing succeeds, they say, like success. And certainly, nothing fails like failure.

—Anon.

Nothing fails like success.

—G. K. Chesterton

Notice the difference between what happens when a man says to himself, "I have failed three times" and what happens when he says "I am a failure."

—S. I. Hayakawa

There is no formula for success. But there is a formula for failure and that is trying to please everybody.

—Man Ray

Men were born to succeed, not to fail.

—Henry David Thoreau

See SUCCESS

Faith

Faith: is belief without evidence to what is told by he who speaks without knowledge of things without parallel.

—*Ambrose Bierce*

Martyrs create faith, more than faith creates martyrs.

—*Miguel de Unamuno*

Every truth has two faces, every rule two surfaces, every precept two applications.

—*Petrus Jacobus Joubert*

Faith is under the left nipple.

—*Martin Luther*

The word "orthodoxy" not only no longer means not being right, it practically means being wrong.

—*G. K. Chesterton*

The greatest act of faith is when man decides he is not God.

—*Oliver Wendell Holmes*

Christ died for our sins. Dare we make his martyrdom meaningless by not committing them.

—*Jules Feiffer*

Without faith, a man can do nothing; with it, all things are possible.

—*William Osler*

I could prove God statistically.

—*George Gallup*

I do not consider it an insult, but rather a compliment to be called an agnostic. I do not pretend to know where many ignorant men are sure—that is all that agnosticism means.

—*Clarence Darrou*

He does not believe that does not live according to his belief.

—*Thomas Fuller*

The success of any venture will be helped by prayer, even in the wrong denomination.

—*Anon.*

Earth is an oasis in the heart which will never be reached by the caravan of thinking.

—*Kahlil Gibran*

If a man have a strong faith he can indulge in the luxury of skepticism.

—*Friedrich Wilhelm Nietzsche*

See BIBLE, GOD

Fame

Wealth is like sea-water; the more we drink, the thirstier we become and the same is true of fame.

—*Arthur Schopenhauer*

A root is a flower that disdains fame.

—*Kahlil Gibran*

Popularity is a crime from the moment it is sought; it is only a virtue where men have it whether they will or no.

—*Lord Halifax*

If you would not be forgotten as soon as you are dead, either write things worth reading or do things worth writing.

—*Benjamin Franklin*

If fame is to come only after death, I am in no hurry for it.

—*Martial*

Fame is so sweet that we love anything with which we connect it, even death.

—*Blaise Pascal*

How many people live on the reputation of the reputation they might have made.

—*Oliver Wendell Holmes*

Contempt of fame begets contempt of virtue.

—*Samuel Johnson*

Men shut their doors against a setting sun.

—*William Shakespeare*

Most celebrated men live in a condition of prostitution.

—*Charles-Augustin Sainte-Beuve*

Why long for glory, which one despises as soon as one has it? But that is precisely what the ambitious man wants: having it in order to despise it.

—*Jean Rostand*

See ACHIEVEMENT, ACCOMPLISHMENT, CELEBRITY, SUCCESS

Family

What was silent in the father speaks in the son, and often I have found the son the unveiled secret of the father.

—*Friedrich Wilhelm Nietzsche*

God gives us relations; thank God we can choose our friends.

—*Ethel Mumford*

The family is the nucleus of civilization.

—*Will Durant*

A friend who is near and dear may become as useless as a relative in time.

—*George Ade*

There are no illegitimate children, only illegitimate parents.

—*Leon Yankowich*

No matter how many communes anybody invents, the family always creeps back.

—*Margaret Mead*

The family you come from isn't as important as the family you're going to have.

—*Ring Lardner*

Why pay money to have your family tree traced? Go into politics and your opponents will do it for you.

—*Mark Twain*

Happy families are all alike; every unhappy family is unhappy in its own way.

—*Leo Tolstoy*

See ANCESTRY, CHILDREN, PARENTS

Fanaticism

The weakness of the fanatic is that those whom he fights have a secret hold on him, and to this weakness, he and his group finally succumb.

—*Paul Tillich*

And he goes through life, his mouth open, and his mind closed.

—*Oscar Wilde*

A fanatic is a man that does what he thinks the Lord would do if he knew the facts of the case.

—*Finley Peter Dunne*

Fanaticism consists in redoubling your efforts when you have forgotten your aim.

—*George Santayana*

A fanatic is one who sticks to his guns, whether they're loaded or not.

—*Franklin Jones*

The worst vice of the fanatic is his sincerity.

—*Oscar Wilde*

Fashion

Fashion is that by which the fantastic becomes for the moment the universal.

—*Oscar Wilde*

Fashion, n., a despot whom the wise ridicule and obey.

—*Ambrose Bierce*

Dress is a very foolish thing, and yet, it is a very foolish thing for a man not to be well dressed.

—*Lord Chesterfield*

Fashion is gentility running away from vulgarity and afraid of being overtaken.

—*William Hazlitt*

The time he can spare from the adornment of his person he devotes to the neglect of his duties.

—*Benjamin Jowett*

Woman's first duty in life is to her dress maker. What the second duty is, no one has yet discovered.

—*Oscar Wilde*

A fashion is nothing but an induced epidemic.

—*George Bernard Shaw*

Fashion is a form of ugliness so intolerable that we have to alter it every six months.

—*Oscar Wilde*

See VANITY

I do not believe in a fate that falls on men however they act, but I do believe in a fate that falls on men unless they act.

—*G. K. Chesterton*

Lots of folks confuse management with destiny.

—*Kim Hubbard*

Successful men of action are not sufficiently self-observant to know exactly on what their success depends.

—*J. Jacobs*

Luck affects everything. Let your hook always be cast in the stream where you least expect there will be a fish.

—*Ovid*

The Moving Finger writes; and, having writ,
Moves on: nor all your Piety nor wit
Shall lure it back to cancel half a Line,
Nor all your Tears wash out a Word of it.

—*Omar Khayyam*

See LUCK, OPPORTUNITY

Fear

The only thing we have to fear is fear itself.

—*Franklin D. Roosevelt*

Fear of hypocrites and fools is the great plague of thinking and writing.

—*Jules Gabriel Janin*

We fear something before we hate it. A child who fears noises becomes a man that hates noise.

—*Cyril Connolly*

We have to realize that we are as deeply afraid to live and to love as we are to die.

—*R. D. Laing*

To a man who is afraid, everything rustles.

—*Sophocles*

As cowardly as a coward is, it is not safe to call a coward a coward.

—*Anon.*

Quiet minds cannot be perplexed or frightened but go on in fortune or misfortune at their own private pace, like a clock in a thunderstorm.

—*Robert Louis Stevenson*

To conquer fear is the beginning of wisdom.

—*Bertrand Russell*

Fear cannot be without hope nor hope without fear.

—*Baruch Spinoza*

Whoever is abandoned by hope has also been abandoned by fear; this is the meaning of the word "desperate."

—*Arthur Schopenhauer*

Fear of becoming a has-been keeps some people from becoming anything.

—*Eric Hoffer*

We mustn't fear daylight just because it almost always illuminates a miserable world.

—*René Magritte*

See EMOTION, FEELINGS

Those who do not feel pain seldom think that is is felt.

—*Samuel Johnson*

If merely "feeling good" could decide, drunkenness would be the supremely valid human experience.

—*William James*

No one can make you feel inferior without your consent.

—*Eleanor Roosevelt*

It is harder to hide feelings we have than to feign those we lack.

—*François de La Rochefoucauld*

We feel in one world. We think in another. Between the two, we can set up a series of references, but we cannot fill the gap.

—*Marcel Proust*

See ANGER, BLUSHING, EGO, EMOTIONS, ENVY, FEAR, GRIEF, HATE, HAPPINESS, HOPE, JEALOUSY, LOVE, SORROW

Fighting

You should never wear your best trousers when you go out to fight for liberty and truth.

—Herbert Gibson

There is no squabbling so violent as that between people who accepted an idea yesterday and those who will accept it tomorrow.

—Christopher Morley

War is sweet to those who have not experienced it.

—Erasmus

Whoever battled with monsters had better see that it does not turn him into a monster. And if you gaze long in an abyss, the abyss will gaze back into you.

—Friedrich Wilhelm Nietzsche

An infallible method of conciliating a tiger is to allow oneself to be devoured.

—Konrad Adenauer

War would end if the dead could return.

—Stanley Baldwin

We have the power to make this the best generation of mankind in the history of the world, or the last.

—John F. Kennedy

War is too important to be left to the generals.

—Georges Clemenceau

War is only a cowardly escape from the problems of peace.

—Thomas Mann

There are no warlike peoples, just warlike leaders.

—Ralph Bunche

War can only be abolished through war.

—Mao Zedong

See ANGER, WAR

Film

American motion pictures are written by the half educated for the half witted.

—S. Irvine

It's more than magnificent. It's mediocre.

—*Samuel Goldwyn*

A film is the world in an hour and a half.

—*Jean-Luc Godard*

The film is a machine for seeing more than meets the eye.

—*I. Barry*

Cinema should make you forget you're sitting in a theatre.

—*Roman Polanski*

The cinema is not a slice of life. It's a piece of cake.

—*Alfred Hitchcock*

The trouble with a movie these days is that it is old before it is released. It is no accident that it comes in a can.

—*Orson Welles*

A movie without sex would be like a candy bar without nuts.

—*Earl Wilson*

The cinema has no boundaries.It is a ribbon of dream.

—*Orson Welles*

The cinema is truth twenty-four times a second.

—*Jean-Luc Godard*

A film is a petrified garden of thought.

—*Jean Cocteau*

What we want is a story that starts with an earthquake and works its way up to a climax.

—*Samuel Goldwyn*

See ACTING, HOLLYWOOD

Flattery

Just praise is a debt, but flattery is a present.

—*Samuel Johnson*

Flattery is counterfeit money which, but for vanity, would have no circulation.

—*François de La Rochefoucauld*

He soft-soaped her until she couldn't see for the suds.

—*Mary Roberts Rinehart*

We refute praise from a desire to be praised twice.

—François de La Rochefoucauld

What really flatters a man is that you think him worth flattering.

—George Bernard Shaw

After a man is fifty you can fool him by saying he is smart, but you can't fool him by saying he is pretty.

—E. W. Howe

He who praises you for what you lack wishes to take from you what you have.

—Eugene Manuel

When a man is really important, the worst adviser he can have is a flatterer.

—Anon.

We seek our happiness outside ourselves, and in the opinion of men whom we know to be flatterers, insincere, unjust, full of envy, caprice, and prejudice. How absurd.

—Jean de La Bruyère

Food

Grub first, then ethics.

—*Bertold Brecht*

There is no love sincerer than the love of food.

—*George Bernard Shaw*

For its merit, I will knight it and then it will be Sir-Loin.

—*Charles II*

To eat is human, to digest divine.

—*Mark Twain*

Salt is the policeman of taste; it keeps the various flavors of a dish in order and restrains the stronger from tyrannizing over the weaker.

—*Chazal*

I would like to find a stew that will give me heartburn immediately instead of at three o'clock in the morning.

—*John Barrymore*

Fishes live in the sea as men do a-land; the big ones eat the little ones.

—*Pericles*

Bad men live that they may eat and drink, whereas good men eat and drink that they may live.

—*Socrates*

Gastronomy rules all life: the newborn baby's tears demand the nurse's breast, and the dying man receives with some pleasure the last cooling drink.

—*Anthelme Brillat-Savarin*

Part of the secret of success in life is to eat what you like and let the food fight it out.

—*Mark Twain*

Few among those who go to restaurants realize the man who first opened one must have been a man of genius and a profound observer.

—*Anthelme Brillat-Savarin*

Let me smile with the wise and eat with the rich.

—*Samuel Johnson*

See DIET, HEALTH

Fool

A fellow who is always declaring he's no fool, usually has his suspicions.

—*Anon.*

For fools rush in where angels fear to tread.

—*Alexander Pope*

Let us be thankful for the fools. But for them, the rest of us could not succeed.

—*Robert Frost*

Fortune, seeing that she could not make fools wise, has made them lucky.

—*Michel de Montaigne*

A mother takes twenty years to make a man of her boy, and another woman makes a fool of him in twenty minutes.

—*Robert Frost*

A fool and his father's money can go places.

—*Anon.*

Forgiving

Almost everyone takes pleasure in repaying small obligations; many are thankful for moderate acts of kindness but scarcely anyone is thankful for great mercies.

—*François de La Rochefoucauld*

He who has not forgiven an enemy has not yet tasted one of the most sublime enjoyments of life.

—*Johann Lavater*

Many promising reconciliations have broken down because while both parties came prepared to forgive, neither party came prepared to be forgiven.

—*Anon.*

His heart was as great as the world but there was no room in it to hold the memory of a wrong.

—*Robert Emerson*

See LOVE

The wind is the only thing in civilization to enjoy freedom.

—*Elias Canetti*

A nation may lose its liberties in a day and not miss them for a century.

—*Baron de Montesquieu*

We feel free when we escape, even if it be from the frying pan into the fire.

—*Eric Hoffer*

Liberty is the right to tell people what they do not want to hear.

—*George Orwell*

Freedom is only good as a means; it is no end in itself.

—*Herman Melville*

The basic test of freedom is perhaps less in what we are free to do than in what we are free not to do.

—*Eric Hoffer*

I don't think anyone is free. One creates one's own prison.

—*George Sutherland*

Freedom is indivisible, and when one man is enslaved, all are not free.

—*John F. Kennedy*

Those who expect to reap the blessings of freedom must, like men, undergo the fatigue of supporting it.

—*Thomas Paine*

We are all of us the worse for too much liberty.

—*Anon.*

A hungry man is not a free man.

—*Adlai Stevenson*

To be free is to have achieved your life.

—*Tennessee Williams*

See LIBERTY

Friendship

The only safe and sure way to destroy an enemy is to make him your friend.

—*Mark Twain*

There is little friendship in the world and least of all between equals.

—*Francis Bacon*

Friend: one who knows all about you and loves you just the same.

—*Elbert Hubbard*

Without friends, the world is but a wilderness.

—*Francis Bacon*

A real friend is one who walks in when the rest of the world walks out.

—*Walter Winchell*

A true friend is the most precious of all possessions and the one we take least thought about acquiring.

—*François de La Rochefoucauld*

Friendship may, and often does, grow into love, but love never subsides into friendship.

—*Lord Byron*

So long as we love we serve; so long as we are loved by others, I would almost say that we are indispensable; and no man is useless while he has a friend.

—*Robert Louis Stevenson*

Life is to be fortified by many friendships. To love, and to be loved, is the greatest happiness of existence.

—*Sydney Smith*

Never speak ill of yourself; your friends will always say enough on that subject.

—*Charles de Talleyrand-Perigord*

It is not so much our friends' help that helps us as the confident knowledge that they will help us.

—*Epicurus*

There are three faithful friends—an old wife, an old dog, and ready money.

—*Benjamin Franklin*

Life without a friend, death without a witness.

—*George Herbert*

If there were only two men in the world, how would they get on? They would help one another, harm one another, flatter one another, slander one another, fight one another, make it up; they could neither live together nor do without one another.

—*Voltaire*

Don't go to visit a friend in the hour of his disgrace.

—*Rabbi Ben Eleazer*

Go often to the house of a friend for weeds choke the unused path.

—*Ralph Waldo Emerson*

And if a friend does evil to you, say to him, "I forgive you for what you did to me, but how can I forgive you for what you did to yourself?"

—*Friedich Wilhelm Nietzsche*

Life is not worth living for the man who has not even one good friend.

—*Democritus*

It takes your enemy and your friend, working together, to hurt you to the heart; the one to slander you and the other to get the news to you.

—*Mark Twain*

He makes no friend who never made a foe.

—*Alfred Lord Tennyson*

Hearts that are delicate and kind and tongues that are neither—these make the finest company in the world.

—*Logan Pearsall Smith*

Everybody is not capable of being a friend, but everybody has it in his power to be an enemy.

—*Anon.*

It is easier to forgive an Enemy than to forgive a Friend.

—*William Blake*

How much easier to make pets of our friends' weaknesses than to put up with strengths.

—*Elizabeth Bibesco*

True friendship is never serene.

—*Marquise de Sévigné*

Since we are mortal, friendships are best kept to a moderate level, rather than sharing the very depths of our souls.

—*Euripides*

When a man laughs at his troubles he loses a good many friends. They never forgive the loss of their prerogative.

—*H. L. Mencken*

In prosperity our friends know us; in adversity we know our friends.

—*John Churton Collins*

Of what help is anyone who can only be approached with the right words?

—*Elizabeth Bibesco*

He that has no one to love or confide in, has little to hope. He wants the radical principle of happiness.

—*Samuel Johnson*

It is more shameful to distrust one's friends than to be deceived by them.

—*François de La Rochefoucauld*

We have fewer friends than we imagine, but more than we know.

—*Hugo von Hoffmannsthal*

If the first law of friendship is that it has to be cultivated, the second law is to be indulgent when the first law has been neglected.

—*Voltaire*

Friend is sometimes a word devoid of meaning; *enemy*, never.

—*Victor Hugo*

Enemies publish themselves. They declare war. The friend never has to declare his love.

—*Henry David Thoreau*

See ENEMIES

Future

The future is like heaven—everyone exalts it, but no one wants to go there now.

—*James Baldwin*

The strongest are those who renounce their own times and become a living part of those yet to come. The strongest and the rarest.

—*Milovan Djilas*

We must take care that the forward movement does not degenerate into a headlong run. We must see to it that enthusiasm for the future does not give rise to contempt for the past.

—*Pope Paul VI*

The future is an opaque mirror. Anyone who tries to look into it sees nothing but the dim outlines of an old worried face.

—*Jim Bishop*

The best thing about the future is that it comes one day at a time.

—*Dean Acheson*

This is my prediction for the future—whatever hasn't happened will happen and no one will be safe from it.

—*J. B. S. Haldane*

Everyone's future is, in reality, an urn full of unknown treasures from which all may draw unguessed prizes.

—*Lord Dunsany*

It is bad enough to know the past; it would be intolerable to know the future.

—*W. Somerset Maugham*

We can neither put back the clock nor slow down our forward speed, and as we are already flying pilotless, on instrument controls, it is even too late to ask where we are going.

—*Igor Stravinsky*

The danger of the past was that men became slaves. The danger of the future is that men may become robots.

—Eric Fromm

The future is the past in preparation.

—P. Dac

Between midnight and dawn when sleep will not come and all the old wounds begin to ache, I often have a nightmare vision of the future world in which there are billions of people, all numbered and registered, with not a gleam of genius anywhere, not an original mind, a rich personality, on the whole packed globe. The twin ideas of our time, organization and quantity, will have won forever.

—J. B. Pristeley

I never think of the future; it comes soon enough.

—Albert Einstein

I still lived in the future—a habit which is the death of happiness.

—Quentin Crisp

I like men who have a future and women who have a past.

—Oscar Wilde

I steer my bark with hope ahead and fear astern.

—*Thomas Jefferson*

We should all be concerned about the future because we will have to spend the rest of our lives there.

—*Charles Kettering*

Gambling

One should always play fairly when one has the winning cards.

—*Oscar Wilde*

The roulette table pays nobody except him that keeps it. Nevertheless, a passion for gambling is common, though a passion for keeping roulette tables is unknown.

—*George Bernard Shaw*

There are two times in a man's life when he should not speculate—when he can't afford it, and when he can.

—*Mark Twain*

Gambling promises for the poor what property performs for the rich—something for nothing.

—*George Bernard Shaw*

The gambling known as business looks with severe disfavor on the business known as gambling.

—*Ambrose Bierce*

Genius

Genius may have its limitations, but stupidity is not this handicapped.

—*Elbert Hubbard*

Silence does not always mean wisdom.

—*Samuel Coleridge*

I have nothing to declare but my genius.

—*Oscar Wilde*

When a true genius appears in the world, you know him by this sign, that the dunces are all in confederacy against him.

—*Jonathan Swift*

Sometimes men come by the name of genius in the same way that certain insects come by the name of centipede—not because they have a hundred feet, but because most people can't count above fourteen.

—*George Lichtenberg*

Caricature is the tribute that mediocrity pays to genius.

—*Oscar Wilde*

See TALENT

Giving

You are indeed charitable when you give, and, while giving, turn your face away so that you may not see the shyness of the receiver.

—*Kahlil Gibran*

If the enemy be hungry, give him bread to eat; and if he be thirsty, give him water to drink.

—*Proberbs 25:21*

Take egotism out and you would castrate the benefactors.

—*Ralph Waldo Emerson*

To enjoy a good reputation, give publicly, and steal privately.

—*S. Billinger*

The worst of charity is that the lives you are asked to preserve are not worth preserving.

—*Ralph Waldo Emerson*

We often borrow from our tomorrows to pay our debts
to our yesterdays.

—Kahlil Gibran

One can know nothing of giving aught that is worthy to
give unless one also knows how to take.

—Havelock Ellis

The only gift is a portion of thyself.

—Ralph Waldo Emerson

It is better to deserve without receiving than to receive
without deserving.

—Robert Ingersoll

We like the gift when we the giver prize.

—John Sheffield

You must be fit to give before you can be fit to receive.

—James Stephens

God

This only is denied to God: the power to undo the past.

—Agathon

All things bright and beautiful,
All creatures great and small,
All things wise and wonderful,
The Lord God made them all.

—*Cecil Frances Alexander*

The Ethiopians say that their gods are snub-nosed and black, the Thracians that theirs have light blue eyes and red hair.

—*Xenophanes*

The religions we call false were once true.

—*Ralph Waldo Emerson*

A man cannot become an atheist merely by wishing it.

—*Napoleon*

It's Socrate's opinion, and mine too, that it is best judged of heaven not to judge it at all.

—*Ralph Waldo Emerson*

The words of the prophets are written on the subway walls and tenement halls.

—*Paul Simon, "The Sound of Silence"*

Politics and church are the same thing. They keep the people in ignorance.

—*Anon.*

As the caterpillar chooses the fairest leaves to lay her eggs on, so the priest lays his curse on the fairest joys.

—*William Blake*

God made everything out of nothing. But the nothing-ness shows through.

—*Paul Valéry*

It is hard to believe in God, but it is far harder to disbelieve in him.

—*Harry Emerson Fosdick*

When the missionaries arrived, the Africans had the land, and the missionaries had the Bible; they taught us to pray with our eyes closed. When we opened them, they had the land, and we had the Bible.

—*Jomo Kenyatta*

Of course he [God] will forgive me; that's his business.

—*Heinrich Heine*

Is man one of God's blunders? Or is God one of man's blunders?

—*Friedrich Wilhelm Nietzsche*

If I were a nightingale, I would sing like a nightingale; if a swan like a swan. But, since I am a rational creature, my role is to praise God.

—*Epictetus*

The sufferer alone is permitted to praise God in his works. But all men suffer.

—*Franz Rosenzweig*

I love to pray at sunrise—before the world becomes polluted with vanity and hatred.

—*The Koretser Rabbi*

God was satisfied with his own work, and that is fatal.

—*Samuel Butler*

I respect the idea of God too much to hold it responsible for a world as absurd as this one is.

—*Georges Dumahel*

The impotence of God is infinite.

—*Analote France*

God dwells wherever man lets him in.

—*Mendel of Kotzk*

Live among men as if God beheld you; speak to God as if men were listening.

—*Seneca*

Man considers the actions, but God weighs the intentions.

—*Thomas à Kempis*

God wants the heart.

—*The Talmud*

If God were suddenly condemned to life the life which he has inflicted on men, He would kill Himself.

—*Alexander Dumas fils*

The true way goes over a rope which is not stretched at any great height but just above the ground. It seems more designed to make people stumble than to be walked upon.

—*Franz Kafka*

All religions promise a reward for excellence of the will or heart, but none for excellence of the head or understanding.

—*Arthur Schopenhauer*

Wandering in a forest late at night, I have only a faint light to guide me. A stranger appears and says to me, "My friend, you should blow out your candle in order to find your way more clearly." This stranger is a theologian.

—*Denis Diderot*

Every miracle can be explained—after the event. Not because the miracle is no miracle, but because explanation is explanation.

—*Franz Rosenzweig*

Many a long dispute among divines may be thus abridged: it is so. It is not so. It is so. It is not so.

—Benjamin Franklin

God is a writer, and we are both heroes and the readers.

—Isaac Bashevis Singer

An atheist is a person who has no invisible means of support.

—Fulton J. Sheen

God is a concept by which we measure our pain.

—John Lennon

All gods were immortal.

—Stanislaw Lec

God's contempt for human minds is evidenced by miracles. He judges them unworthy of being drawn to Him by other means than those of stupefaction and the crudest modes of sensibility.

—Paul Valéry

It is very dangerous to go into eternity with possibilities which one has oneself prevented from becoming realities. A possibility is a hint from God.

—Sören Kierkergaard

Man is a dog's ideal of what God should be.

—*Helen Jackson*

One thing is pretty obvious in these days. If the clergy went on strike, society would soon learn to live without them.

—*Jules Jacques*

To what excesses will men not go for the sake of a religion in which they believe so little and which they practice so imperfectly!

—*Jean de La Bruyère*

All religions will pass, but this will remain: simply sitting in a chair and looking in the distance.

—*V. V. Rozanov*

The trees reflected in the river—they are unconscious of a spiritual world so near them. So are we.

—*Nathaniel Hawthorne*

I like the silent church before the service begins, better than any preaching.

—*Ralph Waldo Emerson*

A pious man is one who would be an atheist if the king were.

—*Jean de La Bruyère*

It were better to be of no church than to be bitter for any.

—*William Penn*

A religion, even if it calls itself the religion of love, must be hard and unloving to those who do not belong to it.

—*Sigmund Freud*

You have to be very religious to change your religion.

—*Anon.*

Religion is built on humility; honor on pride. How to reconcile them must be left to wiser heads than mine.

—*Tommy Manville*

Every night, I still ask the Lord, "Why?" and I haven't heard a decent answer yet.

—*Jack Kerouac*

God seems to have left the receiver off the hook and time is running out.

—*Arthur Koestler*

We have no choice but to be guilty. God is unthinkable if we are innocent.

—*Archibald MacLeish*

If on Judgement Day, I was confronted with God and I found God took himself seriously, I would like to go to the other place.

—*Malcolm Muggeridge*

God gives himself to men as powerful or perfect. It is for them to choose.

—*Simone Weil*

Complacency in the presence of miracles is like opening the door to your own tomb.

—*Rod Steiger*

God has not called me to be successful; he has called me to be faithful.

—*Mother Theresa*

He who knows about depth, knows about God.

—*Paul Tillich*

See AFTERLIFE, BIBLE, HELL

Goodwill

The most precious thing anyone, man or business, anybody or anything, can have is the good will of others.

—*Anne Parish*

To be good is noble, but to show others how to be good is nobler and no trouble.

—*Mark Twain*

If I knew for a certainty that a man was coming to my house with the conscious design of doing me good, I should run for my life.

—*Henry David Thoreau*

Be not simply good. Be good for something.

—*Henry David Thoreau*

You are not only good yourself, but the cause of goodness in others.

—*Socrates*

See HATE

Every man who takes office in Washington either grows or swells.

—Woodrow Wilson

I can govern the United States or I can govern my daughter, Alice, but I can't do both.

—Theodore Roosevelt

No government can be long secure without formidable opposition.

—Benjamin Disraeli

The best government is not that which renders men the happiest but that which renders the greatest number happy.

—Charles Pinot Duclos

The hardest thing about any political campaign is how to win without proving that you are unworthy in the winning.

—Adlai Stevenson

No man undertakes a trade he has not learned, even the meanest. Yet everyone thinks himself sufficiently qualified for the hardest of all trades, that of government.

—*Socrates*

You cannot extend the mastery of government over the daily working life of people without at the same time making it the master of the people's souls and thoughts.

—*Herbert Hoover*

I feel like the small boy who stubbed his toe; he was too old to cry, and it hurt too much to laugh.

—*Adlai Stevenson*

See DEMOCRACY

Gratitude

Next to ingratitude, the most painful thing is . . . gratitude.

—*Henry Ward Beecher*

Gratitude is when memory is stored in the heart and not in the mind.

—*Lionel Hampton*

Gratitude is a useless word. You will find it in a dictionary but not in life.

—*François de La Rochefoucauld*

He that has satisfied his thirst turns his back on the well.

—*Baltasar Gracián*

Greatness

Great minds have purposes; others have wishes.

—*Washington Irving*

A one-eyed man is king in the land of the blind.

—*Anon.*

He was dull in a new way, and that made many think him great.

—*Samuel Johnson*

The greatest truths are the simplest, and so are the greatest men.

—*Joseph Howe*

An occasional weakness in a great man is a comfort to the rest of us.

—Herbert Prochnow

No great man lives in vain. The history of the world is but the biography of great men.

—Thomas Carlyle

Be not afraid of greatness: some are born great; some achieve greatness, and some have greatness thrust upon them.

—William Shakespeare: Twelfth Night

A great man represents a great ganglion in the nerves of society, or, to vary the figure, a strategic point in the campaign of history, and part of his greatness consists in his being *there*.

—Oliver Wendell Holmes, Jr.

Grief

Excess of grief for the deceased is madness, for it is an injury to the living, and the dead know it not.

—Xenophanes

One can bear brief, but it takes two to be glad.

—*Elbert Hubbard*

It is foolish to tear one's hair in grief, as though sorrow would be made less with baldness.

—*Cicero*

We weep to avoid the shame of not weeping.

—*François de La Rochefoucauld*

It is dangerous to abandon oneself to the luxury of grief: it deprives one of courage, and even of the wish for recovery.

—*Henri Frédéric Amiel*

See SORROW, SUFFERING

Habit

Chaos often breeds life, when order breeds habit.

—*Henry Adams*

Vulgarity is the garlic in the salad of taste.

—*James Brendan Connelly*

The fixity of a habit is generally in direct proportion to its absurdity.

—*Marcel Proust*

I believe that the mind can be permanently profaned by the habit of attending to trivial things so that all our thoughts shall be tinged with triviality.

—*Henry David Thoreau*

Happiness

Happiness: an agreeable sensation arising from contemplating the misery of others.

—*Ambrose Bierce*

It's pretty hard to tell what does bring happiness. Poverty and wealth have both failed.

—*Elbert Hubbard*

There is no happiness that is not idleness and only what is useless is pleasurable.

—*Anton Chekhov*

Extremely happy and extremely unhappy men are alike prone to grow hard hearted.

—*Baron de Montesquieu*

We deem those happy who from the experience of life have learned to bear its ills without being overcome by them.

—*Juvenal*

Happiness is a perfume you cannot pour on others without getting a few drops on yourself.

—*Ralph Waldo Emerson*

Happiness is a perpetual possession of being well deceived.

—*Jonathan Swift*

Most folks are about as happy as they make up their minds to be.

—*Abraham Lincoln*

Happiness is a how, not a what: a talent, not an object.

—*Hermann Hesse*

To be able to throw oneself away for the sake of a moment, to be able to sacrifice years for a woman's smile—that is happiness.

—*Hermann Hesse*

There is an hour wherein a man might be happy all his life, could he find it.

—*George Herbert*

192

One kind of happiness is to know exactly at what point to be miserable.

—*François de La Rochefoucauld*

The only way to avoid being miserable is not to have enough leisure to wonder whether you are happy or not.

—*George Bernard Shaw*

The poor man is happy; he expects no change for the worse.

—*Demetrius*

A happy life is one spent in learning, earning, and yearning.

—*Lillian Gish*

It's good to have money and the things that money can buy but it's good to check up once in a while to make sure you haven't lost the things that money can't buy.

—*George Claude Lorimer*

Happiness grows at our own firesides and is not to be picked in strangers' gardens.

—*D. Jerrard*

The happiest people seem to be those who have no particular reason for being happy except that they are so.

—*William Inge*

There are men who seem to have started off in life with a bottle or two of champagne inscribed to their credit.

—*William James*

Whoever is happy will make others happy too. He who has courage and faith will never perish in misery!

—*Anne Frank*

There is no such thing as the pursuit of happiness, but there is the discovery of joy.

—*J. Grentell*

If we only wanted to be happy, it would be easy; but we want to be happier than other people, and that is almost always difficult, since we think them happier than they are.

—*Baron de Montesquieu*

A large income is the best recipe for happiness I ever heard of.

—*Jane Austen*

The sense of existence is the greatest happiness.

—*Benjamin Disraeli*

No man is happy; he is at best fortunate.

—Solon

See EMOTION

Hardship

A cobweb is as good as the mightiest cable when there is no strain upon it.

—Henry Ward Beecher

Adversity is the first path to truth.

—Anon.

The times are not so bad as they seem; they couldn't be.

—Anon.

Half a calamity is better than a whole one.

—T. E. Lawrence

Adversity reminds men of religion.

—Livy

No pain, no palm; no thorns, no throne; no gall, no glory; no cross, no crown.

—*William Penn*

Hate

He that fears you present will hate you absent.

—*Thomas Fuller*

Hate is always a clash between our spirit and someone else's body.

—*Cesare Pavese*

Great fury, like great whiskey, requires long fermentation.

—*Truman Capote*

You know what they say: the sweetest word in the English language is revenge.

—*P. Beard*

Let them hate, so long as they fear.

—*Lucius Accius*

Now hatred is by far the longest pleasure;
Men love in haste, but they detest at leisure.

—*Lord Byron*

Friends may come and go, but enemies accumulate.

—*T. Jones*

Like the greatest virtue and the worst dogs, the fiercest hatred is silent.

—*Jean Paul Richter*

Impotent hatred is the most horrid of all emotions; one should hate nobody whom one cannot destroy.

—*Johann Wolfgang von Goethe*

If a man say, I love God, and hateth his brother, he is a liar. He that loveth not his brother whom he hath seen, how can he love God whom he hath not seen?

—*1 John 4:20*

See EMOTION, LOVE

Health

The art of medicine consists of amusing the patient while nature cures the disease.

—Voltaire

To safeguard one's health at the cost of too strict a diet is a tiresome illness indeed.

—François de La Rochefoucauld

Illness is a great leveler. At its touch, the artificial distinctions of society vanish away. People in a hospital are just people.

—M. Thorek

A man who is "of sound mind" is one who keeps the inner madman under lock and key.

—Paul Valéry

There's lots of people who spend so much time watching their health, they haven't time to enjoy it.

—Josh Billings

Wisdom is to the soul what health is to the body.

—De Saint-Real

Health is infinite and expansive in mode, and reaches out to be filled with the fullness of the world; whereas the disease is finite and reductive in mode, and endeavors to reduce the world to itself.

—Anon.

The body never lies.

—Martha Graham

Your body is the baggage you must carry through life. The more excess baggage the shorter the trip.

—A. Glasgow

If you want to live, you must walk. If you want to live long, you must run.

—J. Navik

Heart

The nearest to my heart are a king without a kingdom and a poor man who does not know how to beg.

—Kahlil Gibran

If you look into your own heart, you find nothing wrong there; what is there to worry about? What is there to fear?

—Confucius

199

The mother's heart is the child's school room.

—*Henry Ward Beecher*

The world either breaks or hardens the heart.

—*Nicolas Chamfort*

Hell

He did not think it was necessary to make a hell of this world to enjoy paradise in the next.

—*William Beckford*

I never did give anyone hell. I just told the truth, and they thought it was hell.

—*Harry Truman*

The road to hell is paved with good intentions.

—*Karl Marx*

Hell, madame, is to love no longer.

—*Georges Bernanos*

I believe in heaven and hell, on earth.

—*Abraham Feinberg*

Men have fiendishly conceived a heaven, only to find it insipid, and a hell only to find it ridiculous.

—*George Santayana*

See AFTERLIFE, BIBLE, GOD

Heroism

As you get older, it is harder to have heroes, but it is sort of necessary.

—*Ernest Hemingway*

We can't all be heroes because someone has to sit on the curb and clap as they go by.

—*Will Rogers*

I still think the movie heroes are in the audience.

—*Wilson Mizner*

I never thought much of the courage of a lion tamer. Inside the cage, he is at least safe from people.

—*George Bernard Shaw*

To bear other people's afflictions, everyone has courage and enough to spare.

—*Benjamin Franklin*

Being a hero is about the shortest lived profession on earth.

—*Will Rogers*

Kill reverence and you have killed the hero in a man.

—*Edward Rand*

In war, the heroes always outnumber the soldiers ten to one.

—*H. L. Mencken*

One of our American wits said that it took only half as long to train an American army as any other because you only had to train them to go one way.

—*Woodrow Wilson*

History

The main thing is to make history, not to write it.

—*Otto von Bismarck*

Perhaps in time the so-called dark ages will be thought of as including our own.

—*Georg Christoph Lichtenberg*

Men, after death are understood worse than men of the moment, but heard better.

—*Friedrich Wilhelm Nietzsche*

We are the children of our age, but children who can never know their mother.

—*Lillian Smith*

The greatest inventions were produced in the times of ignorance, as the use of the compass, gunpowder, and printing.

—*Jonathan Swift*

Very few things happen at the right time, and the rest do not happen at all. The conscientious historian will correct these defects.

—*Herodotus*

The certainties of one age are the problems of the next.

—*R. H. Tawney*

In these new towns, one can find the old houses only in people.

—*Emanuel Canete*

Makes of men date, like makes of cars.

—*Elizabeth Bowen*

Just as philosophy is the study of other people's misconceptions, so history is the study of other people's mistakes.

—*Phillip Guedalla*

Do not seek to follow in the footsteps of the men of old; seek what they sought.

—*Matsuo Basho*

To give an accurate description of what never happened is the proper occupation of the historian.

—*Oscar Wilde*

Our ignorance of history makes us libel our own times. People have always been like this.

—*Gustave Flaubert*

God can not alter the past, but historians can.

—*Samuel Butler*

By despising all that has preceded us, we teach others to despise ourselves.

—*William Hazlitt*

The one thing that does not change is that at any and every time it appears that there have been "great changes."

—*Marcel Proust*

Men are more like the times they live in than they are like their fathers.

—*Ali Ibn-Abi-Talib*

History knows no resting places and no plateaus.

—*Henry Kissinger*

The history of humankind is a repository of scuttled objective truths and a museum of irrefutable facts, refuted not by empirical discoveries, but by man's mysterious decisions to experience differently from time to time.

—*Friedrich Heller*

The man who sees two or three generations is like someone who sits in a conjurer's booth at a fair and sees the tricks two or three times. They are meant to be seen only once.

—*Arthur Schopenhauer*

History books that contain no lies are extremely dull.

—*Anatole France*

Throughout history the world has been laid waste to ensure the triumph of conceptions that are now as dead as the men that died for them.

—*Henry De Montherlant*

What is amusing now had to be taken in desperate earnest once.

—Virginia Woolf

Each generation imagines itself to be more intelligent than the one that went before it and wiser than the one that comes after it.

—George Orwell

Ask counsel of the Ancients, what is best; but of the Moderns, what is fittest.

—Thomas Fuller (II)

The greatest of men are always linked to their age by some weakness or other.

—Johann Wolfgang von Goethe

The people who live in a Golden Age usually go around complaining how yellow everything looks.

—Randall Jarrell

The novelties of one generation are only the resuscitated fashions of the generation before last.

—George Bernard Shaw

It takes time to ruin a world, but time is all it takes.

—Bernard Fontenelle

All history is the propaganda of the victorious.

—Anon.

Those who cannot remember the past are condemned to repeat it.

—George Santayana

History: an account mostly false of events unimportant which are brought about by rulers mostly knaves and soldiers mostly fools.

—Ambrose Bierce

In analyzing history, do not be too profound, for often the causes are quite superficial.

—Ralph Waldo Emerson

Hollywood

Millions are to be grabbed out here and your only competition is idiots.

—Herbert Mankiewicz

No matter how hot it gets in the daytime in Hollywood it's always dull at night.

—Sam Marx

You're only as good as your last picture.

—*Sam Marx*

Audiences will reach for quality but never stoop.

—*Irving Thalberg*

You can have the best producer and the best director but it won't make any difference if you don't have the story.

—*Marie Dressler*

It's slave labor and what do you get for it? A lousy fortune!

—*S. N. Behrman*

Nobody sets out to make a bad picture.

—*Anon.*

Tragedy is death at the box office.

—*Louis B. Mayer*

A verbal contract isn't worth the paper it's written on.

—*Samuel Goldwyn*

There's nothing wrong with this business that a good picture won't cure.

—*Nicholas M. Schenk*

See ACTING, TELEVISION

Hope

"Blessed is the man who expects nothing, for he shall never be disappointed." was the ninth beatitude.

—*Alexander Pope*

A cathedral, a wave of a storm, a dancer's leap, never turn out to be as high as we had hoped.

—*Marcel Proust*

We are all in the gutter, but some of us are looking at the stars.

—*Oscar Wilde*

The most absurd and the most rash hopes have sometimes been the cause of extraordinary success.

—*Marquis de Vauvenargues*

If you do not hope, you will not find what is beyond your hopes.

—*St. Clement*

Hope is itself a species of happiness and perhaps the chief happiness which this world affords.

—*Samuel Johnson*

Vows begin when hope dies.

—*Leonardo Da Vinci*

Our hopes, often though they deceive us, lead us pleasantly along the path of life.

—*François de la Rochefoucauld*

Honor begets honor; trust begets trust; faith begets faith, and hope is the mainspring of life.

—*Henry L. Stimson*

Hope is generally a wrong guide, though it is very good company by the way.

—*Lord Halifax*

Hope is a good breakfast, but it is a bad supper.

—*Francis Bacon*

Men should do with their hopes as they do with tame foul: cut their wings that they may not fly over the wall.

—*Lord Halifax*

The natural flights of the human mind are not from pleasure to pleasure, but from hope to hope.

—*Samuel Johnson*

The sudden disappointment of a hope leaves a scar which the ultimate fulfillment of that hope never entirely removes.

—*Thomas Hardy*

We often call a certainty a hope, to bring it luck.

—*Elizabeth Bibesco*

Second marriage: the triumph of hope over experience.

Samuel Johnson

Hope is a waking dream.

—*Aristotle*

See EMOTIONS, FEELINGS, OPTIMISM

My way of joking is telling the truth; that is the funniest joke in the world.

—*George Bernard Shaw*

If you want to make people weep, you must weep yourself. If you want to make people laugh, your face must remain serious.

—*Casanova*

Everything is funny as long as it is happening to somebody else.

—*Will Rogers*

It's hard to be funny if you have to be clean.

—*Mae West*

Jesters do oft prove prophets.

—*William Shakespeare: King Lear*

Sentimental irony is a dog that bays at a moon while he pisses on a grave.

—*Craus*

We must laugh at a man to avoid crying for him.

—*Napoleon*

Fun I love, but too much fun is of all things the most loathsome. Mirth is better than fun, and happiness is better than humor.

—*William Blake*

See LAUGHTER

Husbands

The better the workman, the worse husband.

—*Thomas Draxe*

Wives, submit yourselves unto your own husbands, as unto the Lord. For the husband is the head of the wife, even as Christ is the head of the church . . .

—*Ephesians 5:22—23*

Serve your husband as your master, and beware of him as a traitor.

—*Michel de Montaigne*

A light wife doth make a heavy husband.

> —*William Shakespeare: Merchant of Venice*

Thy husband is thy lord, thy life, thy keeper.

> —*William Shakespeare: The Taming of the Shrew*

The calmest husbands make the stormiest wives.

> —*Thomas Dekker*

He knows little who will tell his wife all he knows.

> —*Thomas Fuller*

There are few women so perfect that their husbands do not regret having married them at least once a day.

> —*Jean de La Bruyère*

A man must ask his wife's leave to thrive.

> —*John Ray*

Upon a man and his wife a husband's infidelity is nothing.

> —*Samuel Johnson*

A husband and wife ought to continue so long united as they love each other.

> —*Percy Bysshe Shelley*

Husband and wife come to look alike at last.

—*Oliver Wendell Holmes*

A man should be taller, older, heavier, uglier, and hoarser than his wife.

—*E. W. Howe*

One can always recognize women who trust their husbands. They look so thoroughly unhappy.

—*Oscar Wilde*

Husbands are like fires. They go out if unattended.

—*Zsa Zsa Gabor*

Do married men make the best husbands?

—*James Gibbons Huneker*

God, give me a rich husband though he be an ass.

—*Thomas Fuller*

There is only one thing to do for a man who is married to a woman who enjoys spending money, and that is to enjoy earning it.

—*E. W. Howe*

Grandchildren don't make a man feel old; it's the knowledge that he's married to a grandmother.

—*G. Norman Collie*

A husband is what is left of a man after the nerve is extracted.

—*Helen Rowland*

See **MARRIAGE, WIVES**

Hypocrisy

I despise the pleasure of pleasing people whom I despise.

—*Michel de Montaigne*

Clean your finger before you point at my spots.

—*Benjamin Franklin*

Man is the only animal that can remain on friendly terms with the victims he intends to eat.

—*Samuel Butler*

I have seen hypocrisy that was so artful that it was good judgment to be deceived by it.

—*Josh Billings*

Hypocrisy is the homage that vice pays to virtue.

—*François de La Rochefoucauld*

Is it not possible to eat me without insisting that I sing the praises of my devourer?

—*Feador Dostoevsky*

Few men speak humbly of humility, chastely of chastity, skeptically of skepticism.

—*Blaise Pascal*

The value of an idea has nothing to do with the success of the man who expresses it.

—*Oscar Wilde*

You can't eat your friends and have them too.

—*Bud Schulberg*

Be on your guard against those who confess as their weaknesses all the cardinal virtues.

—*Lord Chesterfield*

With people of limited ability, modesty is merely honesty, but with those who possess great talent, it is hypocrisy.

—*Arthur Schopenhauer*

Many kiss the hand they wish cut off.

—*George Herbert*

No man is a hypocrite in his pleasures.

—*Samuel Johnson*

See LYING

Ideals

An idealist is one who, on noticing that a rose smells better than a cabbage, concludes that it will also make better soup.

—*H. L. Mencken*

When they come downstairs from their Ivory Tower, idealists are apt to walk straight into the gutter.

—*Logan Pearsall Smith*

When a man forgets his ideals, he may hope for happiness, but not till then.

—*John Oliver Hobbes*

Idealism increases in direct proportion to one's distance from the problem.

—*John Galsworthy*

The idealist is incorrigible. If he is turned out of his heaven, he makes an ideal of his hell.

—*Friedrich Wilhelm Nietzsche*

In our ideals we unwittingly reveal our vices.

—*Jean Rostand*

See BELIEFS

Ideas

The ruling ideas of each age have ever been the ideas of its ruling class.

—*Karl Marx*

It is not in the power of the most exalted wit or enlarged understanding, by any quickness of variety of thought, to invent or frame one new simple idea.

—*John Locke*

That fellow seems to me to possess but one idea, and that is a wrong one.

—*Samuel Johnson*

It is the idea, the feeling and the love God means mankind should strive for and show forth.

—*Robert Browning*

The power of vested interests is vastly exaggerated compared with the gradual encroachment of ideas.

—*John Maynard Keynes*

What's the big idea?

—*Anon.*

The river of truth is always splitting up into arms which reunite. Islanded between them, the inhabitants argue for a lifetime as to which is the mainstream.

—*Cyril Connolly*

Nothing is more dangerous than an idea when it's the only one we have.

—*Alain (Emile Chartier)*

An idea that is not dangerous is unworthy of being called an idea at all.

—Don Marquis

It seems as though I had not drunk of the cup of wisdom but had fallen into it.

—Sören Kierkegaard

A man is infinitely more complicated than his thoughts.

—Paul Valéry

The wise only possess ideas; the greater part of mankind is possessed by them.

—Anon.

Ideas must work through the brains and arms of men, or they are no better than dreams.

—Ralph Waldo Emerson

A powerful idea communicates some of its power to the man who contradicts it.

—Marcel Proust

To accept an unorthodoxy is always to inherit unresolved contradictions.

—George Orwell

The idea wants changelessness and eternity. Whoever lives under the supremacy of the idea strives for permanence; hence, everything that pushes toward change must be against it.

—*Carl Jung*

Folly is our constant companion throughout life; if someone appears wise, it is only because his follies are suited to his age and station.

—*François de La Rochefoucauld*

Having ideas is like having chessmen moving forward; they may be beaten, but they may start a winning game.

—*Johann Wolfgang von Goethe*

The history of thought may be summed up in these words: it is absurd by what it seeks, great by what it finds.

—*Paul Valéry*

When he was expected to use his mind, he felt like a right-handed person who has to do something with his left.

—*Georg Chrisoph Lichtenberg*

See THOUGHT

There is no pleasure in having nothing to do; the fun is in having lots to do and not doing it.

—*J. Raper*

It is impossible to enjoy idling thoroughly unless one has plenty of work to do.

—*Jerome K. Jerome*

A loafer always has the correct time.

—*Kin Hubbard*

To be idle and to be poor have always been reproaches and therefore every man endeavors with his utmost care to hide his poverty from others and his idleness from himself.

—*Samuel Johnson*

Weariness has no pain equal to being all rested up with nothing to do.

—*Henry Hoskins*

It is difficult to keep quiet if you have nothing to do.

—*Arthur Schopenhauer*

Work with some men is as besetting a sin as idleness with others.

—*Samuel Butler*

Ennui has made more gamblers than avarice, more drunkards than thirst, and perhaps as many suicides as despair.

—*Charles Caleb Colton*

Every man is or hopes to be, an idler.

—*Samuel Johnson*

An idler is a watch that wants both hands, as useless if it goes as if it stands.

—*William Cowper*

See LAZINESS

Ignorance

Ignorance is ignorance; no right to believe anything can be derived from it.

—*Sigmund Freud*

A silly remark can be made in Latin as well as in Spanish.

—*Miguel de Cervantes*

He that knows little often repeats it.

—*Thomas Fuller*

Ignorance is the necessary condition of life itself. If we knew everything, we could not endure existence for a single hour.

—*Anatole France*

There is an ABC ignorance which precedes knowledge and doctoral ignorance which comes after it.

—*Michel de Montaigne*

I would rather have my ignorance than another man's knowledge, because I have so much of it.

—*Mark Twain*

Ignorance is the mother of all evils.

—*Michel de Montaigne*

It is better to know nothing than to know what ain't so.

—*H. W. Shaw*

Ignorance cannot always be inferred from inaccuracy; knowledge is not always present.

—*Samuel Johnson*

The Skeptics that affirmed they knew nothing, even in that opinion confused themselves and thought they knew more than all the world beside.

—*Sir Thomas Browne*

Your ignorance cramps my conversation.

—*Bob Hope*

If you are ignorant, you certainly can get into some interesting arguments.

—*Herbert Prochnow*

I do not approve of anything which tampers with natural ignorance.

—*Oscar Wilde*

Art hath an enemy called Ignorance.

—*Ben Jonson*

Ignorance, madame, pure ignorance.

—*Samuel Johnson*

Even supposing knowledge to be easily attainable, more people would be content to be ignorant than would take even a little trouble to acquire it.

—*Samuel Johnson*

Where ignorance is bliss, 'tis folly to be wise.

—*Thomas Gray*

Ignorance is of a peculiar nature; once dispelled, it is impossible to reestablish it.

—*Thomas Paine*

Nothing is more terrible than ignorance in action.

—*Johann Wolfgang von Goethe*

Ignorance is degrading only when found in company with riches.

—*Arthur Schopenhauer*

That there should one man die ignorant who had capacity for knowledge, this I call a tragedy.

—*Thomas Carlyle*

There are many things of which a wise man might wish to be ignorant.

—*Ralph Waldo Emerson*

Blind and naked Ignorance
Delivers brawling judgments,
unashamed.

—Alfred Lord Tennyson

Ignorance gives one a large range of probabilities.

—George Eliot

A man's ignorance is as much his private property and
as precious in his own eyes as his family Bible.

—Oliver Wendell Holmes

It may be that the ignorant man, alone, has any chance
to mate his life with life.

—Wallace Stevens

That man must be tremendously ignorant: he answers
every question that is put to him.

—Voltaire

To be ignorant of one's ignorance is the malady of the
ignorant.

—Bronson Alcott

See KNOWLEDGE

Imagination

Were it not for imagination, sir, a man would be as happy in the arms of a chambermaid as a duchess.

—*Samuel Johnson*

Without this playing with fantasy no creative work has ever yet come to birth. The debt we owe to the play of imagination is incalculable.

—*Carl Jung*

There is a space between man's imagination and man's attainment that may only be traversed by his longing.

—*Kahlil Gibran*

Imitation

Imitation is the sincerest form of flattery.

—*Charles Caleb Colton*

No man ever yet became great by imitation.

—*Samuel Johnson*

No one ever heard of state freedom; much less did anyone ever hear of state morals. Freedom and morals are the exclusive possession of individuals.

—*Anon.*

People who cannot bear to be alone are generally the worst company.

—*Albert Guinou*

Man cannot long survive without air, water, and sleep. Next in importance comes food. And close on its heels, solitude.

—*Thomas Szasz*

There will never be a really free and enlightened state until the state comes to recognize the individual as a higher and independent power from which all its own power and authority are derived and treats him accordingly.

—*Henry David Thoreau*

To be happy, we must not be too concerned with others.

—*Albert Camus*

See CHARACTER

Independence

I once worked as a salesman and was very independent. I took orders from no one.

—Jacques Barzun

When I was a boy, I used to do what my father wanted. Now I have to do what my boy wants. My problem is: when am I going to do what I want?

—Sam Levinson

Neither the clamor of the mob nor the voice of power will ever turn me by the breadth of a hair from the course I made out for myself guided by such knowledge as I can obtain and controlled and directed by a solemn conviction of right and duty.

—Robert La Follette

Resolve to be thyself and know that he who finds himself loves his misery.

—Matthew Arnold

In heaven an angel is nobody in particular.

—George Bernard Shaw

All men are forced into one of two categories: those with eleven fingers and those without.

—*Ned Rorem*

It astounds us to come upon other egoists, as though we alone have the right to be selfish and to be filled with eagerness to live.

—*Jules Renard*

How glorious it is and how pointed to be an exception.

—*Alfred de Musset*

We all come down to dinner, but each has a room to himself.

—*Walter Bagehot*

Inflation

How is the human race going to survive now that the cost of living has gone up two dollars a quart?

—*W. C. Fields*

The first panacea for a mismanaged nation is inflation of the currency. The second is war. Both bring a temporary prosperity; both bring a permanent ruin.

—*Ernest Hemingway*

The nation is prosperous on the whole, but how much prosperity is there in a hole?

—*Will Rogers*

We have had two chickens in every pot, two cars in every garage, and now we have two headaches for every aspirin.

—*Fiorello H. La Guardia*

Insanity

There is no need to visit a madhouse to find lunatics.

—*Johann Wolfgang von Goethe*

Insanity is hereditary. You can get it from your kids.

—*Sam Levinson*

I sometimes wonder whether our planet is the asylum of our universe for disordered minds.

—*Johann Wolfgang von Goethe*

Only the insane take themselves seriously.

—*Max Beerbohm*

See HEALTH, REASON

Intelligence

All this worldly wisdom was once the unamiable heresy of some wise man.

—*Henry David Thoreau*

Many would be wise if they did not think themselves wise.

—*Baltasar Gracián*

Wit without employment is a disease.

—*Robert Burton*

Wisdom cannot create materials; they are the gifts of nature or chance; her pride is in the use.

—*Edmund Burke*

A man is not necessarily intelligent because he has plenty of ideas any more than he is a good general because he has plenty of soldiers.

—*Nicolas Chamfort*

You should never be clever but when you cannot help it.

—*Richard Fulke Greville*

It is better not to reflect at all than not to reflect enough.

—*Tristan Bernard*

You can not gauge the intelligence of an American by talking with him.

—*Eric Hoffer*

I suppose you could never prove to the mind of the ingenius mollusk that such a creature as a whale was possible.

—*Ralph Waldo Emerson*

A moment's insight is sometimes worth a life's experience.

—*Oliver Wendell Holmes*

At a certain age, some people's minds close up. They live on their intellectual fat.

—*William Lyon Phelps*

Only the shallow know themselves.

—*Oscar Wilde*

There is something in us wiser than our head.

—*Arthur Schopenhauer*

There is nobody so irritating as somebody with less intelligence and more sense than we have.

—*D. Herold*

An intelligent person often talks with his eyes; a shallow man often swallows with his ears.

—*Anon.*

A really intelligent man feels what other men only know.

—*Baron de Montesquieu*

Such is the delight of mental superiority that none on whom nature or study have conferred it would purchase the gifts of fortune by its loss.

—*Samuel Johnson*

The voice of intelligence . . . is drowned out by the roar of fear . . . Most of all it is silenced by ignorance.

—*Karl Menninger*

Merely having an open mind is nothing. The object of opening the mind, as of opening the mouth, is to shut it again on something solid.

—*G. K. Chesterton*

A man's intelligence does not increase as he acquires power. What does increase is the difficulty in telling him so.

—*D. Southerland*

A man should never be ashamed to own that he has been in the wrong, which is but saying, in other words, that he is wiser today than he was yesterday.

—*Alexander Pope*

Some people will never learn anything, for this reason, because they understand everything too soon.

—*Alexander Pope*

The more intelligent one is, the more men of originality one finds. Ordinary people find no difference between men.

—*Blaise Pascal*

It is not enough to have a good mind. The main thing is to use it well.

—*René Descartes*

See **MIND, THOUGHT**

Israel

The only thing chicken about Israel is their soup.

—*Bob Hope*

When peace comes we will perhaps, in time, be able to forgive the Arabs for killing our sons, but it will be harder for us to forgive them for having forced us to kill their sons.

—*Golda Meir*

In Israel, in order to be a realist, you must believe in miracles.

—*David Ben Gurion*

If Moses had been a committee, the Israelites would still be in Egypt.

—*J. Hughes*

We Jews have a secret weapon in our struggle with the Arabs; we have no place to go.

—Golda Meir

When Arthur Balfour launched his scheme for peopling Palestine with Jewish immigrants I am credibly informed that he did not know there were Arabs in the country.

—William Inge

Jealousy

Jealousy is always born with love, but does not always die with it.

—François de La Rochefoucauld

In jealousy there is more self-love than love.

—François de La Rochefoucauld

Yet he was jealous, though he did not show it,
For jealousy dislikes the world to know it.

—Lord Byron

Jealousy is nothing more than the fear of abandonment.

—Anon.

Jealousy is cruel as the grave.

—*Song of Solomon*

O! beware, my lord, of jealousy;
It is the green-eye'd monster which doth mock
The meat it feeds on . . .

—*Shakespeare: Othello*

Plain women are always jealous of their husbands, beautiful women never are. They are always so occupied with being jealous of other women's husbands.

—*Oscar Wilde*

Jealousy, the jaundice of the soul.

—*John Dryden*

Lots of people know a good thing the minute the other fellow sees it first.

—*Job Hedges*

Moral indignation is jealousy with a halo.

—*H. G. Wells*

Envy is a pain of mind that successful men cause their neighbors.

—*Anon.*

See EMOTION, ENVY

Let me tell you the secret that has led me to my goal. My strength lies solely in my tenacity.

—*Louis Pasteur*

Housekeeping ain't no joke.

—*Anon.*

Hamlet's experience simply could not have happened to a plumber.

—*George Bernard Shaw*

So much of what we call management consists in making it difficult for people to work.

—*Peter Drucker*

When you see what some girls marry, you realize how they must hate to work for a living.

—*H. Rouchard*

Let us be grateful to Adam. He cuts us out of the blessing of idleness and won for us the curse of labor.

—*Mark Twain*

Work is the curse of the drinking class.

—Oscar Wilde

Our chief want in life is somebody who shall make us do what we can.

—Ralph Waldo Emerson

Early to rise and early to bed makes a male healthy and wealthy and dead.

—James Thurber

Oh, my soul, do not aspire to immortal life, but exhaust the limits of the possible.

—Pindar

Nothing is worth doing unless the consequences may be serious.

—George Bernard Shaw

The test of a vocation is the love of the drudgery it involves.

—Anon.

My heart bids me do it if I can, and it is a thing possible to do.

—Homer

Yet all men of good will have this in common, that our works, in the end put us to shame, that always we must begin them afresh, and our sacrifice must be eternally renewed.

—*Hermann Hesse*

Pursue, keep up with, circle round and round your life as a dog does with his master's chaise. Do what you love; know your own bone; gnaw at it, bury it, unearth it, and gnaw it still.

—*Henry David Thoreau*

The heart to conceive, the understanding to direct, and the hand to execute.

—*Anon.*

His weariness is that of the gladiator after the combat; his work was the whitewashing of a corner in a state official's office.

—*Franz Kafka*

I must be used, built into the solid fabric of life as far as there is any usable brick in me, and thrown aside when I am used up. It is only when I am being used that I can feel my own existence, enjoy my own life.

—*George Bernard Shaw*

I love work; it fascinates me. I can sit and look at it for hours. I love to keep it by me. The idea of getting rid of it nearly breaks my heart.

—*Jerome K. Jerome*

See WORK

Journeys

One may not reach the dawn save by the path of night.

—*Kahlil Gibran*

Worth seeing? Yes; but not worth going to see.

—*Samuel Johnson*

Travel makes a wise man better but a fool worse.

—*Thomas Fuller*

A man travels the world over in search of what he needs and returns home to find it.

—*George Moore*

Being in a ship is being in jail, with the chance of being drowned.

—*Samuel Johnson*

Only those who will risk going too far can possibly find out how far one can go.

—*T. S. Eliot*

I never travel without my diary. One should always have something sensational to read in the train.

—*Oscar Wilde*

See TRAVEL

Joy

Weeping may endure for a night, but joy cometh in the morning.

—*Psalms 30:5*

On with the dance! let joy be unconfined.

—*Lord Byron*

How terrible is man's estate. There is not one of his joys which does not spring out of some form of ignorance.

—*Honoré de Balzac*

He chortled in his joy.

—*Lewis Carroll*

Joy is a fruit that Americans eat green.

—*Amando Zegri*

There's not a joy the world can give like that it takes away.

—*Lord Byron*

I found more joy in sorrow than you could find in joy.

—*Sara Teasdale*

Joy, whose hand is ever at his lips, bidding adieu.

—*John Keats*

See EMOTION, HAPPINESS

Judgment

Judge not, that ye be not judged.

—Matthew 7:1

Everyone complains of his memory, and no one complains of his judgment.

—François de La Rochefoucauld

Men's judgements are a parcel of their fortunes, and things outward do draw the inward quality after them, to suffer all alike.

—William Shakespeare: Antony and Cleopatra

It is well, when one is judging a friend, to remember that he is judging you with the same godlike and superior impartiality.

—Arnold Bennett

Next to sound judgment, diamonds and pearls are the rarest things in the world.

—Jean de La Bruyère

We easily enough confess to others as to the advantage of courage, strength, experience, activity, and beauty, but an advantage in judgment we yield to none.

—*Michel de La Montaigne*

Do not wait for the last judgment. It takes place every day.

—*Albert Camus*

Don't mind anything that anyone tells you about anyone else. Judge everyone and everything for yourself.

—*Henry James*

Every morning puts a man on trial, and each evening passes judgment.

—*Roy Smith*

Judge a tree from its fruit, not from the leaves.

—*Euripides*

Justice

Be just before you're generous.

—*R. B. Sheridan*

Justice is always violent to the party offending, for every man is innocent in his own eyes.

—*Daniel Defoe*

Let justice be done, though the heavens fall.

—*Lord Mansfield*

Justice is too good for some people and not good enough for the rest.

—*Norman Douglas*

Injustice is relatively easy to bear: what stings is justice.

—*H. L. Mencken*

See LAWS

Kindness

To cultivate kindness is a valuable part of the business of life.

—*Samuel Johnson*

Kind hearts are more than coronets . . .

—*Alfred Lord Tennyson*

One can always be kind to people one cares nothing about.

—*Oscar Wilde*

When kindness has left people, even for a few moments, we become afraid of them, as if their reason had left them.

—*Will Cather*

Not always actions show the man: we find,
Who does a kindness is not therefore kind.

—*Alexander Pope*

The Turks, a cruel people, who nevertheless are kind to beasts and give alms to dogs and birds.

—*Francis Bacon*

You can get more with a kind word and a gun than you can get with a kind word alone.

—*Rachel Carson*

That best portion of a good man's life,
His little, nameless, unremembered acts,
Of kindness and of love.

—*William Wordsworth*

If you're naturally kind, you attract a lot of people you don't like.

—*William Feather*

Do not wait for extraordinary circumstances to do good; try to use ordinary situations.

—*Jean Paul Richter*

Forget injuries; never forget kindness.

—*Confucius*

Kindness: a language that the dumb can speak and the deaf can understand.

—*C. N. Bovée*

Kindness in words creates confidence. Kindness in thinking creates profoundness. Kindness in giving creates love.

—*Lao-Tse*

Wise sayings often fall on barren ground, but a kind word is never thrown away.

—*Sir Arthur Helps*

See GOODWILL

When women kiss, it always reminds me of prize fighters shaking hands.

> —*H. L. Mencken*

Soul meets soul on lover's lips.

> —*Percy Bysshe Shelley*

What lies lurk in kisses.

> —*Heinrich Heine*

Marriage is the miracle that transforms the kiss from a pleasure into a duty.

> —*Helen Rowland*

If you are ever in doubt as to whether or not you should kiss a pretty girl, always give her the benefit of the doubt.

> —*Thomas Carlyle*

See LOVE

Knowledge

If a little knowledge is dangerous, where is the man who has so much as to be out of danger?

—*Thomas Henry Huxley*

The fear of the Lord is the beginning of knowledge . . . .

—*Proverbs 1:7*

Knowledge is power.

—*Francis Bacon*

All knowledge is of itself of some value. There is nothing so minute or inconsiderable that I would not rather know it than not.

—*Samuel Johnson*

An extensive knowledge is needful to thinking people— it takes away the heat and fever; and helps, by widening speculation, to ease the Burden of the Mystery.

—*John Keats*

Knowledge is capable of being its own end.

—*John Henry Cardinal Newman*

Beware of Had I wist.

—14th century proverb

I have taken all knowledge to be my province.

—Francis Bacon

That observation which is called knowledge of the world will be found much more frequently to make men cunning than good.

—Samuel Johnson

Knowledge is of two kinds. We know a subject ourselves, or we know where we can find information upon it.

—Samuel Johnson

A man must carry knowledge with him, if he would bring home knowledge.

—Samuel Johnson

All that we know is, nothing can be known.

—Lord Byron

Few men make themselves masters of the things they write or speak.

—John Selden

What others think of us would be of little moment did it not, when known so deeply, tinge what we think of ourselves.

—*George Santayana*

To the small part of ignorance that we arrange and classify, we give the name knowledge.

—*Ambrose Bierce*

Seeking to know is only too often learning to doubt.

—*Deshoulieres*

Mistakes are their own instructors.

—*Horace*

A man is accepted into a church for what he believes and he is turned out for what he knows.

—*Mark Twain*

Crafty men condemn studies, simple men admire them, and wise men use them.

—*Francis Bacon*

The man who is too old to learn was probably always too old to learn.

—*Henry Haskins*

Knowledge rests not upon truth alone, but upon error also.

—*Carl Jung*

The more unintelligent a man is, the less mysterious existence seems to him.

—*Arthur Schopenhauer*

All that we know is nothing; we are merely crammed waste-paper baskets unless we are in touch with that which laughs at all our knowing.

—*D. H. Lawrence*

A great deal of learning can be packed into an empty head.

—*Karl Kraus*

Know thyself? If I knew myself, I'd run away.

—*Johann Wolfgang von Goethe*

Knowledge is little; to know the right context is much; to know the right spot is everything.

—*Hugo von Hofmannsthal*

Human life is limited, but knowledge is limitless. To drive the limited in pursuit of the limitless is fatal, and to presume that one really knows is fatal indeed!

—*Chuang-Tzu*

Ignorance is the necessary condition of life itself. If we knew everything, we could not endure existence for a single hour.

—*Anatole France*

Although it is dangerous to have too much knowledge of certain subjects, it is still more dangerous to be totally ignorant of them.

—*Columbat*

I am always ready to learn although I do not always like being taught.

—*Winston Churchill*

The chief knowledge that a man gets from reading books is the knowledge that very few of them are worth reading.

—*H. L. Mencken*

See BOOKS, EDUCATION

Language

If the Romans had been obliged to learn Latin, they would never have found time to conquer the world.

—*Heinrich Heine*

My language is the universal whore whom I have to make into a virgin.

—*L. Kraus*

Communication without purpose is artistic masturbation.

—*Rod Steiger*

Syllables govern the world.

—*John Selden*

The coldest word was once a glowing new metaphor.

—*Thomas Carlyle*

The one stream of poetry which is continually flowing is slang.

—*G. K. Chesterton*

Loquacity storms the ear, but modesty takes the heart.

—*Robert South*

If language had been the creation not of poetry but of logic, we should only have one.

—*Friedrich Hebbel*

Words divide us; action unites us.

—*Tupamaros*

One often makes a remark and only later sees how true it is.

—*Ludwig Wittgenstein*

Thanks to words, we have been able to rise above the brutes, and thanks to words, we have sunk to the level of the demons.

—*Aldous Huxley*

The learned fool writes his nonsense in better language than the unlearned, but it is still nonsense.

—*Ben Franklin*

Words differently arranged have a different meaning and meanings differently arranged have a different effect.

—*Blaise Pascal*

One tongue is sufficient for a woman.

—*John Milton*

How can I tell what I think till I see what I say?

> —*E.M. Forster*

Words are loaded pistols.

> —*Jean Paul Sartre*

Words have finished flirting; now they are making love.

> —*André Breton*

Look wise; say nothing, and grunt. Speech was given to conceal thought.

> —*William Osler*

The most precious things in speech are pauses.

> —*Ralph Richardson*

For every man there is something in the vocabulary that would stick to him like a second skin. His enemies have only to find it.

> —*Ambrose Bierce*

Words—so innocent and powerless as they are, as standing in a dictionary, how potent for good and evil they become in the hands of one who knows how to combine them!

> —*Nathaniel Hawthorne*

See BOOKS, READING, TALK, WORDS

Lateness

For better than never is late.

—*Geoffrey Chaucer*

Five minutes! Zounds! I have been five minutes too late all my lifetime!

—*Hannah Cowley*

Though last not least.

—*Edmund Spenser*

Laughter

If we may believe our logicians, man is distinguished from all other creatures by the faculty of laughter.

—*Joseph Addison*

Laughter is not at all a bad beginning for a friendship, and it is far the best ending for one.

—*Oscar Wilde*

Laugh, if thou art wise.

—*Martial*

We must laugh before we are happy, for fear we die before we laugh at all.

—*Jean de la Bruyère*

Laugh not too much; the witty man laughs last.

—*George Herbert*

Who laughed there? By God, I think it was I myself.

—*Doris Lessing*

And if I laugh at any mortal thing,
'Tis that I may not weep.

—*Lord Byron*

I quickly laugh at everything, for fear of having to cry.

—*Pierre de Beaumarchais*

No man who has once heartily and wholly laughed can be altogether irreclaimably bad.

—*Thomas Carlyle*

Laugh, and the world laughs with you;
Weep, and you weep alone.

—*Ella Wheeler Wilcox*

There is so much to laugh at in this vale of tears.

—*Suderman*

Men show their characters in nothing more clearly than in what they think laughable.

—*Johann Wolfgang von Goethe*

A man of parts and fashion is . . . only seen to smile, but never heard to laugh.

—

We laugh but little in our day, but are we less frivolous?

—*Pierre Jean de Beranger*

Wit ought to be a glorious treat, like caviar. Never spread it about like marmalade.

—*Noel Coward*

Laugh at yourself first before anyone else can.

—*Elsa Maxwell*

Comedy is simply a funny way of being serious.

—*Peter Ustinov*

Comedy, like sodomy, is an unnatural act.

—*Marty Feldman*

The most completely lost of all days is the one on which we have not laughed.

—*Nicolas Chamfort*

A laugh, to be joyous, must flow from a joyous heart, for without kindness, there can be no true joy.

—*Thomas Carlyle*

One half of the world laughs at the other, and fools are they all.

—*Baltasar Gracián*

Wit has truth in it; wisecracking is simply calisthenics with words.

—*Dorothy Parker*

A joke is a kind of coitus interruptus between reason and emotion.

—*Arthur Koestler*

A comedian does funny things; a good comedian does things funny.

—*Buster Keaton*

Laughter is much more important than applause. Applause is almost a duty. Laughter is a reward.

—*Carol Channing*

How can there be laughter, how can there be pleasure, when the whole world is burning.

—*The Dhammapada*

I am sure that since I have had the full use of my reason nobody has ever heard me laugh.

—*G. K. Chesterton*

See HUMOR

Laws

Wretches hang that jurymen may dine.

—*Alexander Pope*

Justice is like a train that's nearly always late.

—*Yevgeny Yevtushenko*

I have forgotten more law than you ever knew, but allow me to say, I have not forgotten much.

—*Anon.*

The English laws punish vice; the Chinese laws do more; they reward virtue.

—*Oliver Goldsmith*

265

Laws are like cobwebs, which may catch small flies but let wasps and hornets break through.

—*Jonathan Swift*

Prisons are built with stones of law, brothels with bricks of religion.

—*William Blake*

Law cannot persuade where it cannot punish.

—*Thomas Fuller*

Men would be great criminals did they need as many laws as they make.

—*Charles John Darling*

There must be justice for the accuser as well as for the accused.

—*Robert Mark*

Government can easily exist without laws, but laws cannot exist without government.

—*Bertrand Russell*

A jury consists of twelve persons chosen to decide who has the better lawyer.

—*Robert Frost*

In the Halls of Justice, the only justice is in the halls.

—*Lenny Bruce*

It is the trade of lawyers to question everything, yield nothing, and to talk by the hour.

—*Thomas Jefferson*

The law is fair to all. In its fairness for equality, it forbids the rich as well as the poor to beg in the streets and to steal bread.

—*Anatole France*

It is criminal to steal a purse, daring to steal a fortune, a mark of greatness to steal a crown. The blame diminishes as the guilt increases.

—*Friedrich von Schiller*

Where law ends, tyranny begins.

—*William Pitt*

I would rather search for justice than for certainty.

—*Anon.*

See JUSTICE

Laziness

We make a mistake if we believe that only the violent passions like ambition and love can subdue the others. Laziness for all her languor is nevertheless often mistress; she permeates every aim and action in life and imperceptibly eats away and destroys passions and virtues alike.

—François de La Rochefoucauld

The lazy are always wanting to do something.

—Marquis de Vauvenargues

Failure is not the only punishment for laziness; there is also the success of others.

—Anon.

The really idle man gets nowhere; the perpetually busy does not get much further.

—H. Ogilvie

To loaf is a science; to loaf is to live.

—Honoré de Balzac

By the street of By-and-By, one arrives at the house of never.

—*Miguel de Cervantes*

Procrastination is suicide on the installment plan.

—*Anon.*

Better to work and fail than to sleep one's life away.

—*Jerome K. Jerome*

Know the true value of time: snatch, seize, and enjoy every moment of it. No idleness, no laziness, no procrastination; never put off till tomorrow what you can do today.

—*Lord Chesterfield*

See WORK

Learning

A little learning is a dangerous thing.

—*Alexander Pope*

What we have to learn to do, we learn by doing.

—Aristotle

In doing we learn.

—George Herbert

. . . much learning doth make thee mad.

—Acts 26:24

There is no great concurrence between learning and wisdom.

—Francis Bacon

Learning makes a good man better and an ill man worse.

—Thomas Fuller

It is only when we forget all our learning that we begin to know.

—Henry David Thoreau

The things we know best are the things we haven't been taught.

—Marquis de Vauvenargues

That which anyone has been long learning unwillingly, he unlearns with proportional eagerness and haste.

—William Hazlitt

According as each has been educated, so he repents of or glories in his actions.

—Baruch Spinoza

Who is wise? He who learns from all men, as it is said, from all my teachers have I gotten an understanding.

—Anon.

I pay the schoolmaster but tis the schoolboys that educate my son.

—Ralph Waldo Emerson

In examinations the foolish ask questions that the wise cannot answer.

—Oscar Wilde

The University brings out all abilities, including stupidity.

—Anton Chekov

Experience is a good teacher, but she sends in terrific bills.

—Minna Antrim

I have learned silence from the talkative, toleration from the intolerant, and kindness from the unkind; yet strange, I am ungrateful to those teachers.

—Kahlil Gilbran

Those who are slow to know suppose that slowness is the essence of knowledge.

—*Friedrich Wilhelm Nietzsche*

Doctrine should be such as should make men in love with the lesson and not with the teacher.

—*Francis Bacon*

Precepts, like fomentations, must be rubbed into us— and with a rough hand too.

—*Lord Halifax*

We receive three educations, one from our parents, one from our schoolmaster, and one from the world. The third contradicts all that the first two teach us.

—*Baron de Montesquieu*

If you think education is expensive, try ignorance.

—*Derek Bok*

Education is a state controlled manufactory of echoes.

—*Norman Douglas*

The first problem for all of us, men and women, is not to learn, but to unlearn.

—*Gloria Steinem*

Do you know the difference between education and experience? Education is when you read the fine print, experience is what you get when you don't.

—*Pete Seeger*

See AUTHORS, BOOKS, EDUCATION, WORDS

Leisure

All intellectual improvement arises from leisure.

—*Samuel Johnson*

To be able to fill leisure intelligently is the last product of civilization.

—*Bertrand Russell*

Generally speaking anybody is more interesting doing nothing than doing anything.

—*Gertrude Stein*

The goal of war is peace; of business, leisure.

—*Aristotle*

The wisdom of a learned man cometh by opportunity of leisure; and he that hath little business shall become wise.

—*Ecclesiasticus 38:24*

The most desirable thing in life after health and modest means is leisure with dignity.

—*Cicero*

Leisure is the mother of Philosophy

—*Thomas Hobbes*

A broad margin of leisure is as beautiful in a man's life as in a book.

—*Henry David Thoreau*

The advantage of leisure is mainly that we may have the power of choosing our own work, not certainly that it confers any privilege of idleness.

—*John Lubbock*

If you are losing your leisure, look out. You may be losing your soul.

—*Anon.*

Nothing can exceed the vanity of our existence but the folly of our pursuits.

—*Oliver Goldsmith*

The finest amusements are the most pointless ones.

—*Jacques Chardonne*

Overwork, n. A dangerous disorder affecting high public functionaries who want to go fishing.

—*Ambrose Bierce*

The follies which a man regrets most are those which he didn't commit when he had the opportunity.

—*Helen Rowland*

Most men pursue pleasure with such breathless haste that they hurry past it.

—*Sören Kierkegaard*

See IDLENESS

Letters

I have made this letter longer than usual because I lack the time to make it short.

—*Blaise Pascal*

I have received no more than one or two letters in my life that were worth the postage.

—Henry David Thoreau

. . . not of the letter, but of the spirit; for the letter killeth, but the spirit giveth life.

—2 Corinthians 3:6

The postman is the agent of impolite surprises. Every week we ought to have an hour for receiving letters— and then go and take a bath.

—Friedrich Wilhelm Nietzsche

There are certain people whom one feels almost inclined to urge to hurry up and die so that their letters can be published.

—Christopher Morley

Letters give us great lives at their most characteristic, their most glorious, and their most terrible moments. Here history and biography meet.

—W. Schuster

When a man sends you an impudent letter, sit right down and give it back to him with interest ten times compounded, and then throw both letters in the waste basket.

—Elbert Hubbard

If you are in doubt whether to write a letter or not, don't. And the advice applies to many doubts in life besides that of letter writing.

—*Edward Bulwer-Lytton*

Correspondences are like small clothes before the invention of suspenders; it is impossible to keep them up.

—*Sydney Smith*

See AUTHORS, BOOKS, WORDS

Liberals

A Liberal is a man who will give away everything he doesn't own.

—*F. Dane*

A Liberal is a man too broadminded to take his own side in a quarrel.

—*Barry Goldwater*

Hell hath no fury like a Liberal scorned.

—*Dick Gregory*

A man who has both feet planted firmly in the air can be safely called a Liberal as opposed to the Conservative, who has both feet planted in his mouth.

—Jacques Barzun

The Liberals can understand everything but people who don't understand them.

—Lenny Bruce

A radical thinks two and two make five. A Liberal is more conservative. He knows two and two make four, but he's unhappy about it.

—Herbert Prochnow

See CONSERVATIVE

Liberty

Freedom is not worth having if it does not connote freedom to err.

—Mahatma Gandhi

Marriage is a lottery in which men stake their liberty, and women their happiness.

—De Rieux

Liberty: one of imagination's most precious possessions.

—*Ambrose Bierce*

The God who gave us life gave us liberty at the same time.

—*Thomas Jefferson*

They that give up essential liberty to obtain a little temporary safety deserve neither liberty nor safety.

—*Benjamin Franklin*

See FREEDOM

Life

The art of life is to know how to enjoy a little and to endure much.

—*William Hazlitt*

There is no cure for birth and death save to enjoy the interval.

—*George Santayana*

Man that is born of woman is of few days, and full of trouble.

—*Psalms 90:9*

Life is short, the art long. opportunity fleeting, experience treacherous, judgment difficult.

—*Hippocrates*

Nature has given man no better thing than shortness of life.

—*Pliny the Elder*

The life so short, the craft so long to learn.

—*Geoffrey Chaucer*

O gentlemen, the time of life is short!

—*William Shakespeare: Sonnets*

Our lives are but our marches to our graves.

—*John Fletcher*

The Wine of Life keeps oozing drop by drop, The Leaves of Life keep falling one by one.

—*Omar Khayyam*

. . . all that a man hath will he give for his life.

—*Job 2:4*

Human existence is always irrational and often painful, but in the last analysis it remains interesting.

—*H. L. Mencken*

It's as large as life and twice as natural.

—*Lewis Carroll*

Life is made up of interruptions.

—*W. S. Gilbert*

To be what we are, and to become what we are capable of becoming, is the only end of life.

—*Robert Louis Stevenson*

Welcome O life! I go to encounter for the millionth time the reality of experience and to forge in the smithy of my soul the uncreated conscience of my race.

—*James Joyce*

For life I had never cared greatly,
As worth a man's while.

—*Thomas Hardy*

Life is real! Life is earnest!
And the grave is not its goal;
Dust thou art, to dust returnest,
Was not spoken of the soul.
Tell me not, in mournful numbers,
Life is but an empty dream!
For the soul is dead that slumbers,
And things are not what they seem.

—*Henry Wadsworth Longfellow*

I slept and dreamed that life was beauty,
I woke—and found that life was duty.

—*Ellen Sturgis Hooper*

I went to the woods because I wished to live deliberately, to front only the essential facts of life, and see if I could not learn what it had to teach, and not, when I came to die, discover that I had not lived.

—*Henry David Thoreau*

Life isn't all beer and skittles . . .

—*Thomas Hughes*

One's real life is so often the life that one does not lead.

—*Oscar Wilde*

So this life of man appears for a short space, but of what went before, or what is to follow, we are utterly ignorant.

—*Venerable Bede*

Life's but a walking shadow, a poor player
That struts and frets his hour upon the stage
And then is heard no more; it is a tale
Told by an idiot, full of sound and fury,
Signifying nothing

—*William Shakespeare: Macbeth*

Life is a pure flame, and we live by an invisible sun within us.

—*Sir Thomas Browne*

Life is an incurable disease.

—*Abraham Cowley*

Life is one long process of getting tired.

—*Samuel Butler*

Life is the art of drawing sufficient conclusions from insufficient premises.

—*Samuel Butler*

Life is a joke that's just begun.

—*W. S. Gilbert*

Life is a long lesson in humility.

—*James M. Barrie*

Life's a long headache in a noisy street.

—*John Masefield*

If you stop struggling, then you stop life.

—*Howard Newton*

You live and learn, or you don't live long.

—*Robert Heinlein*

Where life is more terrible than death, it is then the truest valor to dare to live.

—*Sir Thomas Browne*

Life is too short to be little.

—*Benjamin Disraeli*

There is one word which may serve as a rule of practice for all one's life: reciprocity.

—*Confucius*

If life is a grind, use it to sharpen your wits.

—*Anon.*

A useless life is an early death.

—*Johann Wolfgang von Goethe*

The first half of our life is ruined by our parents, the second half by our children.

—*Clarence Darrow*

When life does not find a singer to sing her heart, she produces a philosopher to speak her mind.

—*Kahlil Gibran*

Life is just a bowl of cherries.

—*Song lyric*

Life is made up of sobs, sniffles, and smiles, with sniffles predominating.

—*O. Henry*

Gather ye rosebuds while ye may,
Old time is still aflying.

—*Robert Herrick*

Only a life lived for others is a life worthwhile.

—*Albert Einstein*

Life is easier than you think; all that is necessary is to accept the impossible, do without the indispensable, and bear the intolerable.

—*Kathleen Norris*

His passions make man live; his wisdom merely makes him last.

—*Nicolas Chamfort*

Life can only be understood backwards, but it must be lived forwards.

—*Sören Kierkegaard*

Every man who refuses to accept the conditions of life sells his soul.

—*Charles Baudelaire*

For the good man to realize that it is better to be whole than good is to enter on a straight and narrow path compared to which his previous rectitude was flowery license.

—*Anon.*

Life is not a spectacle or a feast. It is a predicament.

—*George Santayana*

Let your boat of life be light, packed only with what you need—a homely home and simple pleasures, one or two friends worth the name, someone to love and to love you, a cat, a dog, and a pipe or two, enough to eat and enough to wear, and a little more than enough to drink, for thirst is a dangerous thing.

—*Jerome K. Jerome*

Some go through life getting free rides; others pay full fare and something extra to take care of the free riders. Some of the free riders are those who make an art of "knowing the angles"; others are rascals; others lazy, but some really need help and could not ride unless they rode free. I don't spend much time worrying about the free riders, but I am a full-fare man, first and last.

—*D. Sutten*

Life is barren enough, surely with all her trappings; let us, therefore, be cautious how we strip her.

—*Samuel Johnson*

For everything that lives is holy; life delights in life.

—*William Blake*

My candle burns at both ends;
It will not last the night;
But, ah, my foes, and, oh, my friends—
It gives a lovely light.

—*Edna St. Vincent Millay*

Life is just one damned thing after another.

—*attributed to Francis Ward O'Malley*

There is nothing of which men are so fond, and without care, as life.

—*Jean de La Bruyère*

You are the sunshine of my life;
That's why I'll always stay around.

—*Stevie Wonder*

How can you say my life is not a success? Have I not for more than sixty years got enough to eat and escaped being eaten?

—*Logan Pearsall Smith*

The longer I live, the more keenly I feel that whatever was good enough for our fathers is not good enough for us.

—*Oscar Wilde*

What then remains but that we still should cry
For being born, and, being born, to die.

—*Francis Bacon*

Is life worth living? That is a question for an embryo,
not a man.

—*Samuel Butler*

The tragedy of life is not what men suffer, but rather
what they miss.

—*Thomas Carlyle*

Life is short, but it is long enough to ruin any man who
wants to be ruined.

—*Josh Billings*

What is life? It is the flash of a firefly in the night.

—*Blackfeet Indians*

Life is a one-way street, and we are not coming back.

—*Anon.*

To live remains an art which everyone must learn and
which no one can teach.

—*Havelock Ellis*

If life were predictable it would cease to be life and be without flavor.

—*Eleanor Roosevelt*

Fear not that life shall come to an end but rather fear that it shall never have a beginning.

—*John Henry Cardinal Newman*

Fortune is a God and rules men's lives.

—*Aeschylus*

Life in the U.S.A. is a gift.

—*Bruce Springsteen*

How gaily a man wakes in the morning to watch himself keep on dying.

—*Henry Hoskins*

The unexamined life is not worth living.

—*Plato*

Everything in excess! To enjoy the flavor of life, take big bites. Moderation is for monks.

—*Robert Heinlein*

Life, we learn too late, is in the living, in the tissue of each day and hour.

—*Stephen Leacock*

Life, like a mirror, never gives back more than we put into it.

—*Anon.*

To be what we are and to become what we are capable of becoming is the only end of life.

—*Robert Louis Stevenson*

He who only lives wise lives a sad life.

—*Voltaire*

See **DEATH**

Listening

The hearing ear is always found close to the speaking tongue.

—*Ralph Waldo Emerson*

The ear is something we cannot close at will, and we are the poorer for it.

—*E. Brian*

Listening is a very dangerous thing. If one listens, one may be convinced.

—*Oscar Wilde*

The grace of listening is lost if the listener's attention is demanded not as a favor, but as a right.

—*Pliny the Elder*

Take care what you say before a wall, as you cannot tell who may be behind it.

—*Sa'di*

Give every man thy ear, but few thy voice...

—*William Shakespeare: Hamlet*

We have two ears and only one tongue so that we would listen more and talk less.

—*Diogenes*

Listening is the only way to entertain some folks.

—*Kin Hubbard*

I know how to listen when clever men are talking. That is the secret of what you call my influence.

—*Hermann Suderman*

Literature

The chief glory of every people arises from its authors.

—Samuel Johnson

Literature is news that *stays* news.

—Ezra Pound

Literature is language charged with meaning.

—Ezra Pound

That was the chief difference between literature and life. In books, the proportion of exceptional to commonplace people is high; in reality, very low.

—Aldous Huxley

Literature is the orchestration of platitudes.

—Thornton Wilder

For what are the classics but the noblest recorded thoughts of man? They are the only oracles which are not decayed.

—Henry David Thoreau

A great literature is chiefly the product of inquiring minds in revolt against the immovable certainties of the nation.

—H. L. Mencken

See AUTHORS, BOOKS, LEARNING, WORDS

Loneliness

Loneliness ... is and always has been the central and inevitable experience of every man.

—Thomas Wolfe

People who lead a lonely existence always have something on their minds that they are eager to talk about.

—Anton Chekhov

Loneliness is the first thing which God's eye nam'd not good.

—John Milton

I wandered lonely as a cloud ...

—William Wordsworth

So lonely t'was that God himself
Scarce seemed there to be.

—*Samuel Taylor Coleridge*

See EMPTINESS

Love

She lovede Right fro the firste sighte.

—*Geoffrey Chaucer*

No sooner met, but they looked; no sooner looked but
they loved...

—*William Shakespeare: As You Like It*

But to see her was to love her,
Love but her, and love forever.

—*Robert Burns*

To be loved, be lovable.

—*Ovid*

But there's nothing half so sweet in life
As love's young dream

—*Thomas Moore*

If thou must love me, let it be for naught,
Except for love's sake only.

—*Elizabeth Barrett Browning*

Love is blynd.

—*Geoffrey Chaucer*

To be in love is merely to be in a state of perpetual anaesthesia—to mistake an ordinary young man for a Greek god or an ordinary young woman for a goddess.

—*H. L. Mencken*

The fickleness of the women I love is only equaled by the infernal constancy of the women who love me.

—*George Bernard Shaw*

. . . love is strong as death; jealousy is cruel as the grave.

—*Song of Solomon 8:6*

Yet each man kills the thing he loves . . .

—*Oscar Wilde*

Love in young men, for the most part, is not love but simply sexual desire and its accomplishment is its end.

—*Miguel de Cervantes*

O what a heaven is love! O what a hell!

—*Thomas Dekker*

Love is nothing save an insatiate thirst to enjoy a greedily desired object.

—*Michel de Montaigne*

Love is love's reward.

—*John Dryden*

The reduction of the universe to a single being, the expansion of a single being ever to God, this is love.

—*Victor Hugo*

Love is the business of the idle but the idlenesss of the busy.

—*Edward Bulwer-Lytton*

Love is an egoism of two.

—*Antoine de La Sale*

Come live with me and be my love,
And we will all the pleasures prove...

—*Christopher Marlowe*

Will you love me in the good old fashioned way?
When my hair has all turned gray,
Will you kiss me then and say,
That you love me in December as you do in May?

—*James J. Walker*

It is impossible to love and be wise.

—Francis Bacon

It is commonly a weak man who marries for love.

—Samuel Johnson

Love and dignity cannot share the same abode.

—Ovid

They do not love that do not show their love.

—William Shakespeare: The Two Gentlemen of Verona

... the course of true love never did run smooth.

—William Shakespeare: A Midsummer Night's Dream

Love is the only game that is not called on account of darkness.

—Anon.

Love lasteth as long as the money endureth.

—William Caxton

When poverty comes in at doors, love leaps out at windows.

—John Clarke

Next to the coming to a good understanding with a new mistress, I love a quarrel with an old one.

—*Sir George Etherege*

Greater love hath no man than this, that a man lay down his life for his friends.

—*John 15:13*

Love, and a cough, cannot be hid.

—*George Herbert*

There is no love lost between them.

—*17th century expression*

I could not love thee, dear, so much,
Loved I not honor more.

—*Richard Lovelace*

To know her was to love her.

—*Samuel Rogers*

Perhaps they were right in putting love into books . . . Perhaps it could not live anywhere else.

—*William Faulkner*

A pair of star-cross'd lovers.

—*William Shakespeare: Prologue to Romeo and Juliet*

Lovers never get tired of each other because they are always talking about themselves.

—*François de La Rochefoucauld*

All mankind love a lover.

—*Ralph Waldo Emerson*

The head never rules the heart but just becomes its partner in crime.

—*M. McLaughlin*

The only abnormality is the incapacity to love.

—*Anaïs Nin*

Love is composed of so many sensations that something new of it can always be said.

—*St. Prosper*

From the moment it is touched, the heart can not dry up.

—*Louis Bourdaloue*

Like the measles, love is most dangerous when it comes late in life.

—*Anon.*

Love conquers all things except poverty and a toothache.

—*Mae West*

Love is the triumph of imagination over intelligence.

—*H. L. Mencken*

Love is a fan club with only two fans.

—*Anon.*

The history of love would be the history of humanity; it would be a beautiful book to write.

—*Charles Nodier*

One should always be in love. This is the reason one should never marry.

—*Oscar Wilde*

When a lover gives, he demands, and much more than he is given.

—*Anon.*

To live is to love; all reason is against it; instinct is for it.

—*Samuel Butler*

It is an extra dividend when you like the girl you've fallen in love with.

—*Clark Gable*

A man in love is incomplete until he is married. Then he is finished.

—*Zsa Zsa Gabor*

A man falls in love through his eyes, a woman through her ears.

—*W. Wyatt*

You've got to love something enough to kill it.

—*Martin Scorsese*

Love consists in this, that two solitudes protect and touch and greet each other.

—*Rainer Maria Rilke*

They love too much that die for love.

—*John Ray*

Oh, love is real enough, you will find it some day but it has one archenemy, and that is life.

—*Jean Anouilh*

Love is not a matter of counting the years, it's making the years count.

—*W. Smith*

Women love men for their defects; if men have enough of them, women will forgive them everything even their gigantic intellects.

—*Oscar Wilde*

Let your love be stronger than your hate or anger. Learn the wisdom of compromise, for it is better to bend a little than to break.

—*H. G. Wells*

Of all bodies, the heaviest is the woman who has ceased to love.

—*Lemontey*

See EMOTION, HATE

Luck

Diligence is the mother of good fortune.

—*Miguel de Cervantes*

You can take it as understood
That your luck changes only if it's good.

—*Ogden Nash*

Those who mistake their good luck for their merit are inevitably bound for disaster:

—*J. Christopher Herold*

Well, miss, you'll have a sad husband, you have such good luck at cards.

—*Jonathan Swift*

Little is the luck I've had,
And oh, 'tis comfort small
To think that many another lad
Has had no luck at all.

—*A. E. Housman*

See FATE, OPPORTUNITY

Lying

A man had rather have a hundred lies told of him than one truth which he does not wish should be told.

—*Samuel Johnson*

Sin has many tools, but a lie is the handle which fits them all.

—*Oliver Wendell Holmes*

Why would anyone lie? The truth is always more colorful.

—*James Hall*

Man is ice to truth and fire to falsehood.

—*Jean de La Fontaine*

One of the most striking differences between a cat and a lie is that a cat has only nine lives.

—*Finley Peter Dunne*

I do not mind lying, but I hate inaccuracy.

—*Samuel Butler*

No one lies so boldly as the man who is indignant.

—*Friedrich Wilhelm Nietzsche*

There are people who exaggerate so much that they can't tell the truth without lying.

—*Mark Twain*

He who does not need to lie is proud of not being a liar.

—*Friedrich Wilhelm Nietzsche*

A lie with a purpose is one of the worst kind, and the most profitable.

—*Josh Billings*

There are a terrible lot of lies going about the world, and the worst of it is that they're true.

—*Winston Churchill*

A liar begins with making falsehood appear like truth and ends with making truth itself appear like falsehood.

—*William Shenstone*

Convictions are more dangerous enemies of truth than lies.

—*Friedrich Wilhelm Nietszche*

It is hard to tell if a man is telling the truth when you know you would lie if you were in his place.

—*H. L. Mencken*

There are times when lying is the most sacred of duties.

—*Eugène Marian LaBiche*

Matilda told such dreadful lies,
It made one gasp and stretch one's eyes ...

—*Hillaire Belloc*

Ask me no questions, and I'll tell you no fibs.

—*Oliver Goldsmith*

He that tells a lie to save his credit, wipes his mouth with his sleeve to spare his napkin.

—*Sir Thomas Overbury*

He who tells a lie is not sensible of how great a task he undertakes; for he must be forced to invent twenty more to maintain that one.

—*Alexander Pope*

Half the truth is often a great lie.

—*Benjamin Franklin*

The two-faced answer or the plain protective lie.

—*W. H. Auden*

. . . a lie which is half a truth is ever the blackest of lies. . .

—*Alfred Lord Tennyson*

The great masses of the people ... will more easily fall victims to a big lie than to a small one.

—*Adolf Hitler*

The cruelest lies are often told in silence.

—*Robert Louis Stevenson*

See HYPOCRISY

Man

Man is the only animal that laughs and weeps; for he is the only animal that is struck with the difference between what things are, and what they ought to be.

—*William Hazlitt*

Man is a rational animal who always loses his temper when he is called upon to act in accordance with the dictates of reason.

—*Oscar Wilde*

Man is an intelligence in servitude to his organs.

—*Aldous Huxley*

There are many wonderful things in nature, but the most wonderful of all is man.

—*Sophocles*

What a piece of work is a man!

—*William Shakespeare: Hamlet*

So God created man in his own image . . .

—*Genesis 1:27*

There is no animal in the world so treacherous as man.

—*Michel de Montaigne*

I wonder men dare trust themselves with men.

—*William Shakespeare: Timon of Athens*

The greatest enemy to man is man, who, by the devil's instigation, is a wolf, a devil to himself and others.

—*Robert Burton*

Man's inhumanity to man
Makes countless thousands mourn!

—*Robert Burns*

Man is simply the most formidable of all the beasts of prey, and indeed, the only one that preys systematically on its own species.

—*William James*

See BACHELOR, WOMAN

Manners

A man's natural manner best becomes him.

—*Cicero*

... though I am native here
And to the manner born ...

—*William Shakespeare: Hamlet*

Evil communications corrupt good manners.

—*I Corinthians 15:33*

Not only each country, but every city, yea and every vocation hath its own particular decorum.

—*Michel de Montaigne*

For a man by nothing is so well betrayed,
As by his manners.

—*Edmund Spenser*

If a man be gracious, and courteous to strangers, it
shows he is a citizen of the world ...

—*Francis Bacon*

Men's evil manners live in brass; their virtues
We write in water.

—*William Shakespeare: Henry VIII*

Everyone thinks himself well-bred.

—*Anthony Ashley Cooper*

Civility costs nothing and buys everything

—*Lady Mary Wortley Montagu*

Every man of any education would rather be called a
rascal, than accused of deficiency in the graces.

—*Samuel Johnson*

Members are of more importance than laws. Upon
them, in a great measure, the laws depend.

—*Edmund Burke*

Manners . . . a contrivance of wise men to keep fools at a distance.

—*Ralph Waldo Emerson*

Good breeding consists in concealing how much we think of ourselves and how little we think of the other person.

—*Mark Twain*

The great secret is not having bad manners or good manners or any other particular sort of manners, but having the same manners for all human souls.

—*George Bernard Shaw*

Marriage

Marriage, if one will face the truth, is an evil, but a necessary evil.

—*Menander*

It doesn't much signify whom one marries, for one is sure to find next morning that it was someone else.

—*Samuel Rogers*

... the triumph of hope over experience.

—*Samuel Johnson*

In married life three is company and two is none.

—*Oscar Wilde*

Men marry because they are tired; women because they are curious. Both are disappointed.

—*Oscar Wilde*

Her beauty was sold for an old man's gold
She's a bird in a gilded cage.

—*Arthur J. Lamb*

Married women are kept women and they are beginning to find it out.

—*Logan Pearsall Smith*

Remember, it's as easy to marry a rich woman as a poor woman.

—*William Makepeace Thackeray*

All comedies are ended by a marriage.

—*Lord Byron*

Marriage is popular because it combines the maximum of temptation with the maximum of opportunity.

—*George Bernard Shaw*

If it were not for the presents, an elopement would be preferable.

—*George Ade*

It is better to marry than to burn.

—*I Corinthians 7:9*

Many a good hanging prevents a bad marriage.

—*William Shakespeare: Twelfth Night*

See ALIMONY, DIVORCE

Memory

That which is bitter to endure may be sweet to remember.

—*Thomas Fuller*

The true art of memory is the art of attention.

—*Samuel Johnson*

There is not any memory with less satisfaction in it than the memory of some temptation we resisted.

—*James Branch Cabell*

A man's memory may almost become the art of continually varying and misrepresentating his past, according to his interests in the present.

—*George Santayana*

Mind

You should pray for a sound mind in a sound body.

—*Juvenal*

A sound mind in a sound body is a short but full description of a happy state in this world.

—*John Locke*

When the mind's free, the body's delicate.

—*William Shakespeare: King Lear*

The mind is its own place, and in itself,
Can make a heaven of hell, a hell of heaven.

—*John Milton*

What is mind? No matter. What is matter? Never mind.

—*Thomas Hewitt Key*

No, what it [my mind] is really most like is a spider's web, insecurely hung on leaves and twigs, quivering in every wind, and sprinkled with dewdrops and dead flies.

—*Logan Pearsall Smith*

An improper mind is a perpetual feast.

—*Logan Pearsall Smith*

I saw the best minds of my generation destroyed by madness . . .

—*Allen Ginsberg*

See THOUGHT

Money

The love of money is the mother of all evil.

—*Phocylides*

For the love of money is the root of all evil.

—*I Timothy 6:10*

[The rich] are indeed rather possessed by their money than possessors.

—*Robert Burton*

. . . wine maketh merry: but money answereth all things.

—Ecclesiastes 10:19

But it is pretty to see what money will do.

—Samuel Pepys

They say that knowledge is power. I used to think so, but I now know that they meant money.

—Lord Byron

Money is indeed the most important thing in the world; and all sound and successful personal and national morality should have this fact for its basis.

—George Bernard Shaw

The seven deadly sins . . . Food, clothing, firing, rent, taxes, respectability and children. Nothing can lift those seven millstones from man's neck but money; and the spirit cannot soar until the millstones are lifted.

—George Bernard Shaw

Money is like a sixth sense without which you cannot make a complete use of the other five.

—W. Somerset Maugham

See BUSINESS, TAXES

Morality

We know no spectacle so ridiculous as the British public in one of its periodical fits of morality.

—*Thomas Babington Macaulay*

The foundation of morality is to have done, once and for all, with lying.

—*Thomas Henry Huxley*

Veracity is the heart of morality.

—*Thomas Henry Huxley*

I only know that what is moral is what you feel good after and what is immoral is what you feel bad after.

—*Ernest Hemingway*

What is morality in any given time or place? It is what the majority then and there happen to like, and immorality is what they dislike.

—*Alfred North Whitehead*

It is a moral and political axiom that any dishonorable act, if performed by oneself, is less immoral than if performed by someone else who would be less well-intentioned in his dishonesty.

—*J. Christopher Herold*

They teach the morals of a whore, and the manners of a dancing master.

—*Samuel Johnson*

To be a moral man is to obey the traditional maxims of your community without hesitation or discussion.

—*Charles S. Peirce*

Moral indignation is jealousy with a halo.

—*H. G. Wells*

See BIBLE, GOD

Music

If music be the food of love, play on . . .

—*William Shakespeare: Twelfth Night*

Hell is full of musical amateurs. Music is the brandy of the damned.

—*George Bernard Shaw*

There are only two kinds of music; German music and bad music.

—*H. L. Mencken*

It will be generally admitted that Beethoven's Fifth Symphony is the most sublime noise that has ever penetrated into the ear of man.

—*E. M. Forster*

Such sweet compulsion doth in music lie.

—*John Milton*

Music has charms to soothe a savage breast.

—*William Congreve*

And the night shall be filled with music,
And the cares that infest the day,
Shall fold their tents like the Arabs,
And as silently steal away.

—*Henry Wadsworth Longfellow*

As some to church repair,
Not for the doctrine, but the music there.

—*Alexander Pope*

Wagner's music is better than it sounds.

—*Mark Twain*

See ARTS

Thou shalt love thy neighbour as thyself.

—*Leviticus 19:18*

Love your neighbor, yet pull not down your hedge.

—*George Herbert*

It is discouraging to try to be a good neighbor in a bad neighborhood.

—*William R. Castle*

The crop always seems better in our neighbor's field and our neighbor's cow gives more milk.

—*Ovid*

It is good manners which make the excellence of a neighborhood.

—*Confucius*

Nothing makes you more tolerant of a neighbor's noisy party than being there.

—*Franklin P. Jones*

You're never quite sure how you feel about a neighbor until a "For Sale" sign suddenly appears in front of his house.

—*O. A. Battista*

Good fences make good neighbors.

—*Robert Frost*

The impersonal hand of government can never replace the helping hand of a neighbor.

—*Hubert H. Humphrey*

Get acquainted with your neighbor; you might like him.

—*Father H. B. Tierney*

Living next to you is in some ways like sleeping with an elephant. No matter how friendly and even-tempered is the beast, one is affected by every twitch and grunt.

—*Pierre Elliott Trudeau*

What would I do without my neighbor when the grocery store is closed? One-fourth cup of sugar borrowed at a convenient time has saved many a pie, contributed to many a festivity.

—*Dariel Walsh*

Opinion(s)

Opinion is something wherein I go about to give reasons why all the world should think as I think.

—*John Selden*

. . . opinion in good men is but knowledge in the making.

—*John Milton*

Some praise at morning what they blame at night,
But always think the last opinion right.

—*Alexander Pope*

Opinion is ultimately determined by the feelings, and not by the intellect.

—*Herbert Spencer*

The public buys its opinions as it buys its meat, or takes in its milk, on the principle that it is cheaper to do this than to keep a cow. So it is, but the milk is more likely to be watered.

—*Samuel Butler*

The more unpopular an opinion is, the more necessary is it that the holder should be somewhat punctilious in his observance of conventionalities generally.

—*Samuel Butler*

Opportunity

No great man ever complains of want of opportunity.

—*Ralph Waldo Emerson*

A wise man will make more opportunities than he finds.

—*Francis Bacon*

We must take the current when it serves,
Or lose our ventures.

—*William Shakespeare: Julius Caesar*

Who seeks, and will not take when once 'tis offer'd,
Shall never find it more.

—*William Shakespeare: Anthony and Cleopatra*

Time's ancient bawd, Opportunity.

—*William Rowley*

Opportunity. A favorable occasion for grasping a disappointment.

—*Ambrose Bierce*

Wealth in modern societies is distributed according to opportunity; and while opportunity depends partly upon talent and energy, it depends still more upon birth, social position, access to education and inherited wealth; in a word, upon property.

—*Richard H. Tawney*

See LUCK

Optimism

A pessimist is a man who thinks all women are bad. An optimist is a man who hopes they are.

—*Chauncey Depew*

an optimist is a guy
that has never had
much experience.

—*Don Marquis*

The optimist proclaims that we live in the best of all possible worlds; and the pessimist fears this is true.

—*Jean Branch Cabell*

Two men look out through the same bars;
One sees the mud, and one the stars.

—*Frederick Langbridge*

See HOPE

Originality

All good things which exist are the fruits of originality.

—*John Stuart Mill*

Originality does not consist in saying what no one has ever said before, but in saying exactly what you think yourself.

—*J. F. Stephen*

For I fear I have nothing original in me
Excepting Original Sin

—*Thomas Campbell*

He has left off reading altogether, to the great improvement of his originality.

—Charles Lamb

See **CREATIVITY**

Parents

I tell you there's a wall ten feet thick and ten miles high between parent and child.

—George Bernard Shaw

Oh, what a tangled web do parents weave
When they think that their children are naive.

—-Ogden Nash

Happy is the child whose father goes to the devil.

—16th century proverb

Fathers should be neither seen nor heard. That is the only proper basis for family life.

—Oscar Wilde

Like father, like son.

—William Langland

Diogenes struck the father when the son swore.

—*Robert Burton*

Greatness of name in the father oft-times overwhelms the son; they stand too near one another. The shadow kills the growth: so much, that we see the grandchild come more and oftener to be heir of the first.

—*Ben Jonson*

There must always be a struggle between a father and son, while one aims at power and the other at independence.

—*Samuel Johnson*

The best academy, a mother's knee.

—*James Russell Lowell*

The hand that rocks the cradle is the hand that rules the world.

—*William Ross Wallace*

I want a girl just like the girl that married dear old dad.

—*William Dillon*

Momworship has got completely out of hand.

—*Philip Wylie*

See ANCESTRY, FAMILY

Patience

You heavens, give me that patience, patience I need.

> *—William Shakespeare: King Lear*

Patience, the beggar's virtue.

> *—Philip Massinger*

Beware the fury of a patient man.

> *—John Dryden*

Possess your soul with patience.

> *—John Dryden*

There is a point when patience ceases to be a virtue.

> *—Thomas Morton*

Everything comes if a man will only wait.

> *—Benjamin Disraeli*

Learn to labour and to wait.

> *—Henry Wadsworth Longfellow*

All things come round to him who will but wait.

> *—Henry Wadsworth Longfellow*

Patience, that blending of moral courage with physical timidity.

—*Thomas Hardy*

They also serve who only stand and wait.

—*John Milton*

Lord, grant me patience, and I want it right now.

—*Anon.*

See CHARACTER

Peace

Glory to God in the highest, and on earth peace, good will toward men.

—*Luke 2:14*

The peace of God which passeth all understanding . . .

—*Philippians 4:7*

Give peace in our time, O Lord.

—*The Book of Common Prayer*

The most advantageous peace is better than the most just war.

—*Erasmus*

Anything for a quiet life.

—*Thomas Heywood*

Peace hath her victories
No less renowned than war

—*John Milton*

Peace at any price.

—*Alphose de Lamartine*

Peace with honor. I believe it is peace for our time . . .

—*Neville Chamberlain*

See WAR

Pleasure

There is no such thing as pure pleasure; some anxiety always goes with it.

—*Ovid*

Pleasure is the absence of pain.

—Cicero

Pleasure is nothing else but the intermission of pain.

—John Selden

The honest man takes pains and then enjoys pleasures; the knave takes pleasure, and then suffers pain.

—Benjamin Franklin

I can sympathize with people's pains but not with their pleasures. There is something curiously boring about somebody else's happiness.

—Aldous Huxley

Pleasure is very seldom found where it is sought.

—Samuel Johnson

Having now nobody to please, I am little pleased.

—Samuel Johnson

A life of pleasure is the most unpleasant thing in the world.

—Oliver Goldsmith

The last pleasure in life is the sense of discharging our duty.

—William Hazlitt

Life would be very pleasant if it were not for its enjoyments.

—R. S. Surtees

Life would be tolerable were it not for its amusements.

—Sir George Cornewall Lewis

The true pleasure of life is to live with your inferiors.

—W. M. Thackeray

Simple pleasures are the last refuge of the complex.

—Oscar Wilde

All the things I really like to do are either immoral, illegal, or fattening.

—Alexander Woollcott

See HAPPINESS, JOY

Politics

In politics there is no honour.

—Benjamin Disraeli

Politics makes strange bedfellows.

—*Charles Dudley Warner*

Politics. The conduct of public affairs for private advantage.

—*Ambrose Bierce*

The whole aim of practical politics is to keep the populace alarmed (and hence clamorous to be led to safety) by an endless series of hobgoblins.

—*H. L. Mencken*

You cannot adopt politics as a profession and remain honest.

—*Louis McHenry Howe*

Politics are too serious a matter to be left to the politicians.

—*Charles De Gaulle*

All political parties die at last of swallowing their own lies.

—*John Arbuthnot*

See CONSERVATIVE, GOVERNMENT, LIBERAL

Poverty is the Muse's patrimony.

—Robert Burton

There is no man so poor but what he can afford to keep one dog.

—Josh Billings

Poverty is the openmouthed relentless hell which yawns beneath civilized society.

—Henry George

There is no virtue that poverty destroyeth not.

—John Florio

Poverty is no vice, but an inconvenience.

—John Florio

In the prospect of poverty there is nothing but gloom and melancholy; the mind and body suffer together; its miseries bring no alleviations; it is a state in which every virtue is obscured, and in which no conduct can avoid reproach; a state in which cheerfulness is insensibility, and dejection sullenness, of which the hardships are without honor, and the labors without reward.

—Samuel Johnson

Poverty is a great enemy to human happiness.

—*Samuel Johnson*

To be poor and independent is very nearly an impossibility.

—*William Cobbett*

Poverty is a soft pedal upon all branches of human activity, not excepting the spiritual.

—*H. L. Mencken*

Poverty is not a shame, but the being ashamed of it is.

—*Thomas Fuller*

It's no disgrace t' be poor, but it might as well be.

—*Kin Hubbard*

See RICHES

Power

Power tends to corrupt and absolute power corrupts absolutely.

—*Lord Acton*

They who are in highest places, and have the most power, have the least liberty, because they are most observed.

—John Tillotson

Power, like lightning, injures before its warning.

—Calderón

Power is always gradually stealing away from the many to the few, because the few are more vigilant and consistent.

—Samuel Johnson

The only prize much cared for by the powerful is power.

—Oliver Wendell Holmes, Jr.

Wherever I found a living creature, there I found the will to power.

—Friedrich Wilhelm Nietzsche

The lust for power, for dominating others, inflames the heart more than any other passion.

—Tacitus

Unlimited power is apt to corrupt the minds of those who possess it . . .

—William Pitt

Power, like a desolating pestilence,
Pollutes whate'er it touches . . .

—Percy Bysshe Shelley

Praise

Good men hate those who praise them if they praise
them too much.

—Euripides

He that praiseth publickly, will slander privately.

—Thomas Fuller

Faint Praise is Disparagement.

—Thomas Fuller

Damn with faint praise, assent with civil leer . . .

—Alexander Pope

The praise of a fool is more harmful than his blame.

—Jean Pierre Florian

Praises to the unworthy are felt by ardent minds as
robberies of the deserving.

—Samuel Taylor Coleridge

337

I will praise any man that will praise me.

> —*William Shakespeare: Antony and Cleopatra*

Our heartiest praise is usually reserved for our admirers.

> —*François de La Rochefoucauld*

The refusal of praise is a wish to be praised twice.

> —*François de La Rochefoucauld*

Usually we praise only to be praised.

> —*François de La Rochefoucauld*

Fondly we think we honor merit then,
When we but praise ourselves in other men.

> —*Alexander Pope*

Prejudice

Passion and prejudice govern the world.

> —*John Wesley*

Prejudice is never easy unless it can pass itself off for reason.

> —*William Hazlitt*

Prejudice is the reasoning of the stupid.

—*Voltaire*

Prejudices are the props of civilization.

—*André Gide*

We must not allow prejudice to become a barrier to the full and effective use of our greatest national resources— the talents of our people.

—*Lynn A. Townsend*

If a guy's got it, let him give it. I'm selling music, not prejudice.

—*Benny Goodman*

If we were to wake up some morning and find that everyone was the same race, creed and color, we would find some other causes for prejudice by noon.

—*Senator George Aiken*

Prejudice is a raft onto which the shipwrecked mind clambers and paddles to safety.

—*Ben Hecht*

Most men, when they think they are thinking, are merely rearranging their prejudices.

—*Knute Rockne*

See BIGOTRY

Procrastination

Procrastination is the thief of time.

—Edward Young

Never do today what you can do tomorrow. Something
may occur to make you regret your premature action.

—Aaron Burr

procrastination is the
art of keeping
up with yesterday.

—Don Marquis

Reading

I'm quite illiterate, but I read a lot.

—J. D. Salinger

People say that life is the thing, but I prefer reading.

—Logan Pearsall Smith

Then I thought of reading—the nice and subtle happiness of reading ... this joy not dulled by Age, this polite and unpunishable vice, this selfish, serene, life-long intoxication.

—Logan Pearsall Smith

He has left off reading altogether, to the great improvement of his originality.

—Charles Lamb

Read, mark, learn, and inwardly digest.

—The Book of Common Prayer

Reading furnishes our mind only with materials of knowledge; it is thinking makes what we read ours.

—John Locke

Let blockheads read what blockheads write.

—Lord Chesterfield

A man ought to read just as inclination leads him; for what he reads as a task will do him little good.

—Samuel Johnson

There is an implied contract between author and reader.

—*William Wordsworth*

See AUTHORS, BOOKS, EDUCATION, LITERATURE, WORDS

Reality

Cannot bear very much reality.

—*T. S. Eliot*

Chaos is the score upon which reality is written.

—*Henry Miller*

Melancholy and remorse form the deep leaden keel which enables us to sail into the wind of reality.

—*Cyril Connolly*

Man . . . will debauch himself with ideas, he will reduce himself to a shadow if for only one second of his life he can close his eyes to the hideousness of reality.

—*Henry Miller*

There is nothing in words, believe what is before your eyes.

—*Ovid*

The test which the mind applies to every question must be the test of reality; of validity measured through reason by reality. And yet the dogmatists call those weak who choose the harder, the more rigorous way.

—*Dorothy Thompson*

Real life is, to most men, a long second-best, a perpetual compromise between the ideal and the possible.

—*Bertrand Russell*

Reason

The heart has its reasons which reason cannot know.

—*Blaise Pascal*

As reason is a Rebel unto Faith, so Passion unto Reason.

—*Sir Thomas Browne*

It's common for men to give pretended Reasons instead of one real one.

—*Benjamin Franklin*

The man who listens to Reason is lost; Reason enslaves all whose minds are not strong enough to master her.

—*George Bernard Shaw*

See INSANITY, THOUGHT

Reputation

Woe unto you, when all men shall speak well of you!

—*Luke 6:26*

He that hath the name to be an early riser may sleep till noon.

—*James Howell*

Perhaps the most valuable of all human possessions, next to an aloof and sniffish air, is the reputation of being well-to-do.

—*H. L. Mencken*

Be it true or false, what is said about men often has as much influence upon their lives, and especially upon their destinies, as what they do.

—*Victor Hugo*

The easiest way to get a reputation is to go outside the fold, shout around for a few years as a violent atheist or a dangerous radical, and then crawl back to the shelter.

—*F. Scott Fitzgerald*

Revenge

O revenge, how sweet thou art!

—*Ben Jonson*

Revenge is sweet.

—*Thomas Southerne*

Revenge is profitable, gratitude is expensive.

—*Edward Gibbon*

Sweet is revenge—especially to women.

—*Lord Byron*

A man that studieth revenge keeps his own wounds green.

—*Francis Bacon*

See HATE

Riches

He that trusteth in his riches shall fall.

—Proverbs 24:28

Virtue, glory, honor, all things human and divine, are slaves to riches.

—Horace

The way to enrich are many, and most of them foul.

—Francis Bacon

There is pain in getting, care in keeping, and grief in losing riches.

—Thomas Draxe

The embarrassment of riches.

—Voltaire

Riches have wings, and grandeur is a dream.

—William Cowper

Riches are chiefly good because they give us time.

—Charles Lamb

For all you can hold in your cold dead hand
Is what you have given away

—Joaquin Miller

You can never be too thin or too rich.

—Wallis Warfield Simpson

The rich who are unhappy are worse off than the poor who are unhappy; for the poor, at least, cling to the hopeful delusion that more money would solve their problems—but the rich know better.

—Sydney J. Harris

Let me tell you about the very rich. They are different from you and me. They possess and enjoy early, and it does something to them, makes them soft where we are hard, and cynical where we are trustful, in a way, that, unless you were born rich, it is very difficult to understand.

—F. Scott Fitzgerald

I've been rich, and I've been poor. And believe me, rich is better.

—Joe E. Lewis

People who are hard, grasping and always ready to take advantage of their neighbors, become very rich . . .

—George Bernard Shaw

A rich man is nothing but a poor man with money.

—*W. C. Fields*

The man who dies rich . . . dies disgraced.

—*Andrew Carnegie*

Put in its proper place, money is not man's enemy, not his undoing, nor his master. It is his servant, and it must be made to serve him well.

—*Henry C. Alexander*

I have not observed men's honesty to increase with their riches.

—*Thomas Jefferson*

Ready money is Aladdin's lamp.

—*Lord Byron*

Money is sweet balm.

—*Arab proverb*

Even the blind can see money.

—*Chinese proverb*

If you have no money, be polite.

—*Danish proverb*

No man ever had enough money.

—Gypsy proverb

Money has no ears, but it hears.

—Japanese proverb

Make money, money by fair means if you can, if not, by any means money.

—Horace

The art of getting rich consists not in industry, much less in savings, but in a better order, in timeliness, in being at the right spot.

—Ralph Waldo Emerson

It is easier for a camel to go through the eye of a needle, than for a rich man to enter into the kingdom of God.

—Matthew 19:24

See SUCCESS

Right

A fool must now and then be right, by chance.

—*William Cowper*

I would rather be right than be President.

—*Henry Clay*

Let us have faith that right makes might...

—*Abraham Lincoln*

God's in his heaven
All's right with the world!

—*Robert Browning*

Always do right. This will gratify some people, and astonish the rest.

—*Mark Twain*

When all goes right and nothing goes wrong?
And isn't your life extremely flat
With nothing whatever to grumble at.

—*W. S. Gilbert*

The need to be right—the sign of a vulgar mind.

—*Albert Camus*

See VIRTUE

Security

Only those means of security are good, are certain, are lasting, that depend on yourself and your own vigor.

—*Nicolò Machiavelli*

It is much more secure to be feared than to be loved.

—*Niccolò Machiavelli*

Distrust and caution are the parents of security.

—*Benjamin Franklin*

Some sense of security is necessary to happy or healthful living, but you cannot get it by refusing to take chances any more than a country can get it by living behind walls.

—*Lawrence Gould*

If all that Americans want is security they can go to prison.

—Dwight D. Eisenhower

The most secure individual in our society is a prisoner serving a life sentence.

—Senator Joseph Ball

The tendency is to be broadminded about other people's security.

—Aristide Briand

Self

Self-confidence is the first requisite to great undertakings.

—Samuel Johnson

Trust thyself; every heart vibrates to that iron string.

—Ralph Waldo Emerson

Self-preservation is the first law of nature.

—Samuel Butler

It is a poor center of a man's actions, himself.

—*Francis Bacon*

He that is giddy thinks the world turns round.

—*William Shakespeare: The Taming of the Shrew*

We talk little, if we do not talk about ourselves.

—*William Hazlitt*

He is a poor creature who does not believe himself to be better than the world. No matter how ill we may be, or how low we may have fallen, we would not change identity with any other person. Hence our self-conceit sustains and always must sustain us till death takes us and our conceit together so that we need no more sustaining.

—*Samuel Butler*

We reproach people for talking about themselves; but it is the subject they treat best.

—*Anatole France*

Know thyself.

—*Inscribed on the temple at Delphi*

A man is least known to himself.

—*Cicero*

To know oneself, one should assert oneself.

—*Albert Camus*

Who finds himself, loses his misery!

—*Matthew Arnold*

Who in the world am I? Ah, that's the great puzzle.

—*Lewis Carroll*

See EGO

Sex

Who says two sexes aren't enough?

—*Samuel Hoffenstein*

There is no greater nor keener pleasure than that of bodily love—and none which is more irrational.

—*Plato*

Tis the Devil inspires this evanescent ardor, in order to divert the parties from prayer.

—*Martin Luther*

When we will, they won't; when we don't want to, they want to exceedingly.

—*Terence*

All this humorless document (the Kinsey Report) really proves is; (a) that all men lie when they are asked about their adventures in amour and (b) that pedagogues are singularly naive and credulous creatures.

—*H. L. Mencken*

Women, observing that her mate went out of his way to make himself entertaining, rightly surmised that sex had something to do with it. From that she logically concluded that sex was recreational rather than procreational.

—*James Thurber and E. B. White*

See LOVE, MARRIAGE

Silence

There is no reply so sharp as silent contempt.

—*Michel de Montaigne*

Silence is one great art of conversation.

—*William Hazlitt*

Silence may be as variously shaded as speech.

—*Edith Wharton*

There is an eloquent silence: it serves sometimes to approve, sometimes to condemn; there is a mocking silence, there is a respectful silence.

—*François de La Rochefoucauld*

The world would be happier if men had the same capacity to be silent that they have to speak.

—*Baruch Spinoza*

"Speech is silvern, Silence is golden"; or, as I might rather express it, speech is of time, silence is of eternity.

—*Thomas Carlyle*

See TALK

Sincerity

A little sincerity is a dangerous thing, and a great deal of it is absolutely fatal.

—*Oscar Wilde*

It is dangerous to be sincere unless you are also stupid.

—*George Bernard Shaw*

Love of talking about ourselves and displaying our faults in the light of which we wish them to be seen is the chief element in our sincerity.

—*François de La Rochefoucauld*

See HYPOCRISY

Solitude

Whoever is delighted in solitude is either a wild beast or a god.

—*Francis Bacon*

A man, alone, is either a saint or a devil.

—*Robert Burton*

Who can enjoy alone?

—*John Milton*

It is not good that the man should be alone . . .

—*Genesis 2:18*

357

The happiest of all lives is a busy solitude.

>—*Voltaire*

I never found the companion that was so companionable as solitude.

>—*Henry David Thoreau*

Solitude: A good place to visit, but a poor place to stay.

>—*Josh Billings*

Solitude: a luxury of the rich.

>—*Albert Camus*

See LONELINESS

Sorrow

This is my last message to you: in sorrow seek happiness.

>—*Feodor Dostoevsky*

. . . in sorrow thou shalt bring forth children . . .

>—*Genesis 3 : 16*

More in sorrow than in anger.

>—*William Shakespeare: Hamlet*

When sorrows come, they come not single spies,
But in battalions.

—William Shakespeare: Hamlet

Sorrows are like thunderclouds. Far off they look black,
but directly over us merely gray.

—Jean Paul Richter

Some natural sorrow, loss, or pain,
That has been, and may be again.

—William Wordsworth

See GRIEF

Success

Success or failure lies in conformity to the times.

—Niccolò Machiavelli

I have always observed that to succeed in the world one
should seem a fool, but be wise.

—Baron de Montesquieu

359

Be commonplace and creeping and you will be a success.

—*Pierre de Beaumarchais*

Success has ruined many a man.

—*Benjamin Franklin*

Nothing suceeds like success.

—*Alexander Dumas pere*

Success—"the bitch-goddess Success," in William James's phrase—demands strange sacrifices from those who worship her.

—*Aldous Huxley*

The toughest thing about success is that you've got to keep on being a success. Talent is only a starting point in this business.

—*Irving Berlin*

See CONFIDENCE, CELEBRITY, TALENT

Suffering

By suffering comes wisdom.

—*Aeschylus*

It is not true that suffering ennobles the character; happiness does that sometimes, but suffering, for the most part, makes men petty and vindictive.

—*W. Somerset Maugham*

He's truly valiant who can suffer wisely.

—*William Shakespeare: Timon of Athens*

No pain, no palm; no thorns, no throne; no gall, no glory; no cross, no crown.

—*William Penn*

No pain—no gain.

—*Anon.*

Man, the bravest of the animals and the one most inured to suffering.

—*Friedrich Wilhelm Nietzsche*

To suffer and to endure is the lot of humanity.

—*Pope Leo XIII*

Know how sublime a thing it is
To suffer and be strong.

—*Henry Wadsworth Longfellow*

Over the long run, he who suffers, conquers.

—*Anon.*

To live is also to suffer.

—*Mary Roberts Rinehart*

Man cannot remake himself without suffering. For he is
both the marble and the sculptor.

—*Alexis Carrel*

Misfortunes one can endure—they come from outside,
they are accidents. But to suffer for one's own faults—
ah—there is the sting of life.

—*Oscar Wilde*

Misfortune and suffering is the only true international
currency the world has ever had.

—*Max Wylie*

Grief can take care of itself, but to get the full value of joy you must have somebody to divide it with.

—*Mark Twain*

See GRIEF, SORROW

Talent

Genius must have talent as its complement and implement.

—*Samuel Taylor Coleridge*

Every natural power exhilarates; a true talent delights the possessor first.

—*Ralph Waldo Emerson*

In this world people have to pay an extortionate price for any exceptional gift whatever.

—*Willa Cather*

There is no substitute for talent. Industry and all virtues are of no avail.

—*Aldous Huxley*

It's a great talent to be able to conceal one's talents.

—*François de La Rochefoucauld*

I think this is the most extraordinary collection of talent, of human knowledge, that has ever been gathered together at the White House, with the possible exception of when Thomas Jefferson dined alone.

—*John F. Kennedy*

See ACTING, FILM, HOLLYWOOD, TELEVISION

Talk and Talking

Though I'm anything but clever,
I could talk like that for ever

—*W. S. Gilbert*

A gossip is one who talks to you about others: a bore is one who talks to you about himself: a brilliant conversationalist is one who talks to you about yourself.

—*Lisa Kirk*

Talking is a disease of age.

—*Ben Jonson*

So much they talked, so very little said.

—*Charles Churchill*

We talk little, if we do not talk about ourselves.

—*William Hazlitt*

See SILENCE

Taste

Every one as they like, as the woman said when she kissed her cow.

—*Rabelais*

You had no taste when you married me.

—*Richard Brinsley Sheridan*

Taste is the *only* morality . . . Tell me what you like, and I'll tell you what you are.

—*John Ruskin*

You can't get high aesthetic tastes, like trousers, ready made.

—*W. S. Gilbert*

A man of great common sense and good taste, meaning thereby a man without originality or moral courage.

—*George Bernard Shaw*

Taxes

Taxation without representation is tyranny.

—*James Ottis*

The art of taxation consists in so plucking the goose as to obtain the largest amount of feathers with the least possible amount of hissing.

—*J. B. Colbert*

Taxes are what we pay for civilized society.

—*Oliver Wendell Holmes, Jr.*

There is one difference between a tax collector and a taxidermist—the taxidermist leaves the hide.

—*Mortimer Caplan*

... in this world nothing is certain but death and taxes.

—*Benjamin Franklin*

See **BUSINESS**

Television

Television is the source of our most powerful collective memories.

—*Michael Winshop*

Television is the world's most global language.

—*Michael Winshop*

Television is a kind of radio which lets people at home see what the studio audience is not laughing at.

—*Fred Allen*

My idea of a good television mystery is one where it's hard to detect the sponsor.

—*Irv Lieberman*

Television: Summer stock in an iron lung.

—*Beatrice Lillie*

Television in its present form . . . [is] the opiate of the people of the United States.

—*Richard Nixon*

I hate television. I hate it as much as peanuts. But I can't stop eating peanuts.

—*Orson Welles*

You have debased [my] child. You have made him a laughing stock of intelligence . . . a stench in the nostrils of the ionosphere.

—*Lee DeForest*

The doors to public proceedings should be opened to television whenever they are open to other elements of the press.

—*Robert W. Sarnoff*

Chewing gum for the eyes.

—*John Mason Brown*

See ACTING, HOLLYWOOD

. . . lead us not into temptation . . .

—Matthew 6:13

Watch ye and pray, lest ye enter into temptation. The spirit truly is ready, but the flesh is weak.

—Mark 14:38

There are several good protections against temptations, but the surest is cowardice.

—Mark Twain

Do you really think that it is weakness that yields to temptations? I tell you that there are terrible temptations which it requires strength, strength and courage, to yield to.

—Oscar Wilde

I can resist everything except temptation.

—Oscar Wilde

The only way to get rid of a temptation is to yield to it.

—Oscar Wilde

Never resist temptation: prove all things: hold fast that which is good.

—*George Bernard Shaw*

The last temptation is the greatest treason:
To do the right deed for the wrong reason.

—*T. S. Eliot*

Thought

A penny for your thoughts.

—*Jonathan Swift*

Perish the thought!

—*Colley Cibber*

Great thoughts come from the heart.

—*Marquis de Vauvenargues*

When a thought is too weak to be expressed simply, it is a proof that it should be rejected.

—*Marquis de Vauvenargues*

Strange thoughts beget strange deeds.

—Percy Bysshe Shelley

In fact, it is as difficult to appropriate the thoughts of others as it is to invent.

—Ralph Waldo Emerson

Among mortals second thoughts are the wisest.

—Euripides

The thoughts that come often unsought, and, as it were, drop into the mind, are commonly the most valuable of any we have.

—John Locke

First thoughts are best, being those of generous impulse; whereas Second Thoughts are those of Selfish Prudence.

—Edward Fitzgerald

To think is to live.

—Cicero

I think, but I dare not speak.

—William Shakespeare: Macbeth

I think, therefore I am [Cogito, ergo sum].

—René Descartes

Yon Cassius has a lean and hungry look;
He thinks too much: such men are dangerous.

—William Shakespeare: Julius Caesar

See REASON

Time

Time flies. [Tempus fugit].

—Ovid

My days are swifter than a weaver's shuttle . . .

—Job 7:6

For thogh we slepe or wake, or rome, or ryde,
Ay fleeth the thyme, it nyl no man abyde.

—Geoffrey Chaucer

I hate all times, because all times do fly
So fast away, and may not stayed be.

—Edmund Spenser

Time rolls his ceaseless course.

—Sir Walter Scott

Consider, Sir, how insignificant this will appear a twelve-month hence.

—*Samuel Johnson*

See **AGE**

Travel

The scull is no traveler; the wise man stays at home. Traveling is a fool's paradise.

—*Ralph Waldo Emerson*

It is not worth while to go round the world to count the cats in Zanzibar.

—*Henry David Thoreau*

To travel hopefully is a better thing than to arrive.

—*Robert Louis Stevenson*

Always roaming with a hungry heart.

—*Alfred Lord Tennyson*

I have traveled a good deal in Concord.

—*Henry David Thoreau*

I travel not to go anywhere, but to go.

—*Robert Louis Stevenson*

Everywhere is nowhere. When a person spends all his time in foreign travel, he ends by having many acquaintances, but no friends.

—*Seneca*

See JOURNEYS

Troubles

This I know—if all men should take their trouble to market to barter with their neighbors, not one when he had seen the troubles of other men but would be glad to carry his own home again.

—*Herodotus*

Man is born unto trouble, as the sparks fly upward.

—*Job 5:7*

Man that is born of a woman is of few days, and full of trouble.

—*Job 14:1*

It is pleasant to recall past troubles.

—*Cicero*

Double, double, toil and trouble;
Fire burn and cauldron bubble.

—*William Shakespeare: Macbeth*

The only incurable troubles of the rich are the troubles
that money can't cure, which is a kind of trouble that is
even more troublesome if you are poor.

—*Ogden Nash*

Trust

Trust him no further than you can throw him.

—*Thomas Fuller*

Never trust the man who hath reason to suspect that you
know he hath injured you.

—*Henry Fielding*

It is better to suffer wrong than to do it, and happier to
be sometimes cheated than not to trust.

—*Samuel Johnson*

It is better never to trust anybody.

—*Henrik Ibsen*

Trust, like the soul, never returns, once it is gone.

—*Publilius Syrus*

See BELIEF

Understanding

...get wisdom; and with all thy getting get understanding.

—*Proverbs 4:7*

To understand everything makes one very indulgent.

—*Madame de Stael*

Universe

The universe is one of God's thoughts.

—*Friedrich von Schiller*

Taken as a whole, the universe is absurd.

—*Walter Savage Landor*

...listen: there's a hell
of a good universe next door; let's go.

—*E. E. Cummings*

The universe begins to look more like a great thought
than like a great machine.

—*Sir James Jeans*

Know that you are a part of the whole scheme of
things—a part of the universe.

—*Buckminster Fuller*

See WORLD

Vanity

Vanity, vanity, all is vanity
That's any fun at all for humanity.

—*Ogden Nash*

I have seen all the works that are done under the sun; and behold, all is vanity and vexation of spirit.

—*Ecclesiastes 1:14*

What makes the vanity of other people insupportable is that it wounds our own.

—*François de La Rochefoucauld*

Vanity, like murder, will out.

—*Hannah Cowley*

Life without vanity is almost impossible.

—*Leo Tolstoy*

One will rarely err if extreme actions be ascribed to vanity, ordinary actions to habit, and mean actions to fear.

—*Friedrich Wilhelm Nietzsche*

Cruelty was the vice of the ancient, vanity is that of the modern world. Vanity is the last disease.

—*George Moore*

See EGO

Vice

What were once vices are now the manners of the day.

—*Seneca*

Vice may be had at all prices.

—*Sir Thomas Browne*

We are often saved from exclusive addiction to a single vice by the possession of others.

—*François de La Rochefoucauld*

When the vices give us up, we flatter ourselves that we are giving up them.

—*François de La Rochefoucauld*

The greatest part of human gratifications approach nearly to vice.

—*Samuel Johnson*

I prefer an accommodating vice to an obstinate virtue.

—*Molière*

VICE

Vice is a waste of life. Poverty, obedience, and celibacy are the canonical vices.

—*George Bernard Shaw*

See CRIME, EVIL, VIRTUE

Virtue

Virtue is its own reward.

—*John Dryden*

(Cicero, Seneca, Ovid, Philo, Claudian, Carlyle, and Emerson also expressed this hackneyed aphorism.)

Virtue is a kind of health, beauty and good habit of the soul.

—*Plato*

Virtue is like a rich stone—best plain set.

—*Francis Bacon*

A virtue to be serviceable must, like gold, be alloyed with some commoner but more durable metal.

—*Samuel Butler*

Virtue is the compensation to the poor for the want of riches.

—Horace Walpole

Be good, and you will be lonesome.

—Mark Twain

Virtue itself of vice must pardon beg.

—William Shakespeare: Hamlet

Some rise by sin, and some by virtue fall.

—William Shakespeare: Measure for Measure

In social life, we please more often by our vices than our virtues.

—François de La Rochefoucauld

Our virtues are most frequently but the vices in disguise.

—François de La Rochefoucauld

If he does really think there is no distinction between virtue and vice, why, sir, when he leave our houses let us count our spoons.

—Samuel Johnson

Virtue, enlightened, can be as calculating as vice.

—Honoré de Balzac

Assume a virtue, if you have it not.

—William Shakespeare: Hamlet

See CRIME, EVIL

War

War must be for the sake of peace.

—Aristotle

Peace itself is war in masquerade.

—John Dryden

There never was a good war or a bad peace.

—Benjamin Franklin

To be prepared for war is one of the most effectual means of preserving peace.

—George Washington

See FIGHTING, PEACE

Wife

He that hath wife and children hath given hostages to fortune; for they are impediments to great enterprises, either of virtue, or mischief.

—*Francis Bacon*

It is a good horse than never stumbles,
And a good wife than never grumbles.

—*John Ray*

Whoso findeth a wife findeth a good thing.

—*Proverbs 18:22*

My dear, my better half.

—*Sir Philip Sidney*

Man's best possession is a loving wife.

—*Robert Burton*

The only comfort of my life
Is that I never yet had wife

—*Robert Herrick*

To take a wife merely as an agreeable and rational companion will commonly be found to be a grand mistake.

—*Lord Chesterfield*

Wives are young men's mistresses, companions for middle age, and old men's nurses.

—*Francis Bacon*

What a pity it is that nobody knows how to manage a wife but a bachelor.

—*George Colman the Elder*

The real business of a fall is to look out for a wife, to look after a wife, or to look after somebody else's wife.

—*R. S. Surtees*

See HUSBAND, MARRIAGE

Wisdom

Wisdom never lies.

—*Homer*

The price of wisdom is above rubies.

—Job 28:18

Wisdom is early to despair.

—Gerard Manley Hopkins

One may almost doubt if the wisest man has learned anything of absolute value by living.

—Henry David Thoreau

The only medicine for suffering, crime, and all the other woes of mankind, is wisdom.

—Thomas Henry Huxley

The fear of the Lord is the beginning of wisdom.

—Psalms 111:10

All human wisdom is summed up in two words—wait and hope.

—Alexandre Dumas, pere

A woman is like a tea bag. You don't know her strength until she is in hot water.

—*Nancy Reagan*

Woman is like the reed, which bends in every breeze, but breaks not in the tempest.

—*Richard Whately*

Women prefer us to say a little evil of them, rather than say nothing at all.

—*Louis Xavier de Ricard*

Woman: one of nature's agreeable blunders.

—*Hannah Cowley*

There are two ways to handle a woman, and nobody knows either of them.

—*Kim Hubbard*

Women deserve to have more than twelve years between the ages of twenty-eight and forty.

—*James Thurber*

Woman is unrestrainable, unguidable, intractable, undrawable, unleadable, harsh, bitter, austere, and implacable.

—*Menander*

One is not born a woman; one becomes one.

—*Simone De Beauvoir*

When the candles are out all women are fair.

—*Plutarch*

Like all young men, you greatly exaggerate the difference between one young woman and another.

—*George Bernard Shaw*

For the Colonel's Lady an' Judy O'Grady
Are sisters under their skins!

—*Rudyard Kipling*

Woman would be more charming if one could fall into her arms without falling into her hands.

—*Ambrose Bierce*

Woman was God's *second* mistake.

—*Friedrich Wilhelm Nietzsche*

One can find women who have never had one love affair, but it is rare indeed to find any who have had only one.

—*François de La Rochefoucauld*

But every woman is at heart a rake.

—*Alexander Pope*

In your amours you should prefer old women to young ones. They are so grateful!!

—*Benjamin Franklin*

The two divinest things this world has got,
A lovely woman in a rural spot

—*Leigh Hunt*

. . . can't live with them, or without them.

—*Aristophanes*

Lady, you are the cruel'st she alive.

—*William Shakespeare: Twelfth Night*

Once a woman has given you her heart, you can never get rid of the rest of her.

—*Sir John Vanbrugh*

Let us look for the woman.

—*Alexander Dumas, pere*

See MAN, MARRIAGE

Words

Of all cold words of tongue or pen
The worst are these: "I knew him when"

—*Arthur Guiterman*

Words are, of course, the most powerful drug used by mankind.

—*Rudyard Kipling*

"The question is," said Alice, "whether you *can* make
  words mean so many different things."
"The question is," said Humpty Dumpty, "which is
  to be master—that's all."

—*Lewis Carroll*

How forcible are right words!

—*Job 6:25*

A blow with a word strikes deeper than a blow with a sword.

—Robert Burton

See AUTHOR, BOOKS, DISAPPOINTMENT, EDUCATION, LEARNING, LITERATURE

Work

All work and no play makes Jack a dull boy.

—James Howell

Work keeps us from three great evils, boredom, vice and need.

—Voltaire

All work, even cotton spinning, is noble; work is alone noble.

—Thomas Carlyle

Blessed is he who has found his work; let him ask no other blessedness.

—Thomas Carlyle

For men must work, and women must weep,
And there's little to earn and many to keep...

—*Charles Kingsley*

Work consists of whatever a body is *obliged* to do... Play
consists of whatever a body is not obliged to do.

—*Mark Twain*

Work expands to as to fill the time available for its
completion and the thing to be done swells in importance and complexity in a direct ratio with the time
to be spent.

—*C. Northcote Parkinson*

You may tempt the upper classes
With your villainous demitasses,
But Heaven will protect the working girl.

—*Edgar Smith*

See AMBITION, SUCCESS

The world, which took but six days to make, is like to take six thousand to make out.

—*Sir Thomas Browne*

This may not be the best of all possible worlds, but to say that it is the worst is mere petulant nonsense.

—*T. H. Huxley*

... the world, the flesh, and the devil.

—*The Book of Common Prayer*

O brave new world.

—*William Shakespeare: The Tempest*

The world, where much is to be done and little to be known.

—*Samuel Johnson*

To see a world in a grain of sand ...

—*William Blake*

See UNIVERSE

Youth is the best time to be rich, and the best time to be poor.

—*Euripides*

Almost everything that is great has been done by youth.

—*Benjamin Disraeli*

No wise man ever wished to be younger.

—*Jonathan Swift*

Youth is wasted on the young.

—*George Bernard Shaw*

When the waitress puts the dinner on the table, the old men look at the dinner. The young men look at the waitress.

—*Gelett Burgess*

Youth's a stuff will not endure.

—*William Shakespeare: Twelfth Night*

Youth is a blunder; manhood a struggle; old age a regret.

—*Benjamin Disraeli*

See CHILDREN

Index of Topics

Ability, 1   *see* Accomplishment, Achievement, Jobs, Work
Accomplishment, 2   *see* Ability, Achievement, Jobs, Work
Achievement, 4   *see* Ability, Accomplishment, Jobs, Work
Acting, 7   *see* Hollywood, Films, Talent, Television
Action, 9   *see* Confidence, Success
Adolescence, 11   *see* Age, Children
Advertising, 13
Advice, 15   *see* Criticism
Afterlife, 16   *see* Bible, God, Hell
Age, 19   *see* Life
Alcohol, 24   *see* Desperation, Emptiness
Alimony, 26   *see* Marriage, Divorce
Americans, 28   *see* England
Ancestry, 29   *see* Family, Parents
Anger, 31   *see* Dispute, Emotion

Animals, 32   *see* Cats, Dogs
Arts, 34   *see* Books, Music
Authors, 37   *see* Books, Education, Learning, Literature, Words

Bachelor, 40   *see* Marriage
Bargains, 42
Beauty, 43
Behavior, 45   *see* Character, Man, Self
Believing, 47   *see* Bible, Christianity, God, Trust
Bible, 49   *see* Afterlife, Christianity, God, Hell
Bigotry, 51   *see* Prejudice
Blacks, 52
Blame, 54
Blindness, 55
Blushing, 56   *see* Emotion
Body, 57   *see* Health
Books, 58   *see* Authors, Education, Learning, Literature, Words
Boredom, 63
Bravery, 65   *see* Confidence

Business, 66   see Taxes

Candor, 68   see Advice,
   Criticism
Cats, 69   see Animals, Dogs
Celebrity, 70   see Fame
Change, 71
Character, 72   see Convictions
Charm, 75
Chastity, 76
Children, 77   see Adolescence,
   Age, Youth
Christianity, 81   see Afterlife,
   Bible, God
Civilization, 82   see Man
Committees, 84
Conceit, 85   see Ego
Confidence, 85   see Action,
   Success
Conformity, 86
Conscience, 87
Conservative, 88   see Liberal
Contentment, 89   see Peace
Conversation, 90   see Talk
Convictions, 92   see Believing
Creativity, 93   see Art, Music,
   Words
Crime, 94   see Evil, Law
Criticism, 96   see Candor,
   Advice

Death, 97   see Afterlife, Life
Debt, 102   see Money
Deception, 103   see Lying
Definitions, 104
Democracy, 105   see
   Government
Deprecation, 107   see Blame
Desire and Longing, 108
Desperation, 109   see Alcohol,
   Emptiness
Diet, 110   see Food, Health
Diplomats, 111   see
   Government
Direction, 112
Disappointment, 113
Disease, 114   see Doctors,
   Health

Dispute, 115   see Anger
Divorce, 117   see Alimony,
   Marriage
Doctors, 118   see Health
Dogs, 119   see Animals, Cats
Drama, 120   see Acting,
   Hollywood, Television
Dreams, 121   see Hope

Education, 122   see Books,
   Learning, Words
Ego, 125   see Emotion
Emotion, 127   see Anger,
   Blushing, Ego, Envy, Fear,
   Feelings, Grief, Happiness,
   Hate, Hope, Jealousy, Love,
   Sorrow
Emptiness, 128   see Alcohol,
   Desperation
Enemies, 129   see Friendship
England, 131
Envy, 132   see Emotion,
   Jealousy
Eternity, 133   see Afterlife,
   Bible, God
Evil, 134   see Crime, Goodwill
Experience, 138

Failure, 140   see Success
Faith, 142   see Bible, God
Fame, 144   see Achievement,
   Accomplishment, Celebrity,
   Success
Family, 146   see Ancestry,
   Children, Parents
Fanaticism, 147
Fashion, 148   see Vanity
Fate, 150   see Luck,
   Opportunity
Fear, 151   see Emotions,
   Feelings
Feelings, 153   see Anger,
   Blushing, Ego, Emotions,
   Envy, Fear, Grief, Hate,
   Happiness, Hope, Jealousy,
   Love, Sorrow
Fighting, 154   see Anger, War

Films, 155   see Acting,
    Hollywood
Flattery, 157
Food, 159   see Diet, Health
Fool, 161
Forgiving, 162   see Love
Freedom, 163   see Liberty
Friendship, 165   see Enemies
Future, 170

Gambling, 173
Genius, 174   see Talent
Giving, 175
God, 176   see Afterlife, Bible,
    Hell
Goodwill, 185   see Hate
Government, 186   see
    Democracy
Gratitude, 187
Greatness, 188
Grief, 189   see Sorrow,
    Suffering

Habit, 190
Happiness, 191   see Emotion
Hardship, 195
Hate, 196   see Emotion, Love
Health, 198
Heart, 199
Hell, 200   see Afterlife, Bible,
    God
Heroism, 201
History, 202
Hollywood, 207   see Acting,
    Television
Hope, 209   see Emotions,
    Feelings, Optimism
Humor, 212   see Laughter
Husbands, 213   see Marriage,
    Wives
Hypocrisy, 216   see Lying

Ideals, 218   see Beliefs
Ideas, 219   see Thought
Idleness, 223   see Laziness
Ignorance, 224   see Knowledge
Imagination, 229

Imitation, 229
Independence, 231
Individualism, 230   see
    Character
Inflation, 232
Insanity, 233   see Health,
    Reason
Intelligence, 234   see Mind,
    Thought
Israel, 238

Jealousy, 239   see Emotion,
    Envy
Jobs, 241   see Work
Journeys, 244   see Travel
Joy, 245   see Emotion,
    Happiness
Judgment, 247
Justice, 248   see Laws

Kindness, 249   see Goodwill
Kiss, 252   see Love
Knowledge, 253   see Books,
    Education

Language, 258   see Books,
    Reading, Talk, Words
Lateness, 261
Laughter, 261   see Humor
Laws, 265   see Justice
Laziness, 268   see Work
Learning, 269   see Authors,
    Books, Education, Words
Leisure, 273   see Idleness
Letters, 275   see Authors,
    Books, Words
Liberal, 277   see Conservative
Liberty, 278   see Freedom
Life, 279   see Death
Listening, 290
Literature, 292   see Authors,
    Books, Learning, Words
Loneliness, 293   see Emptiness
Love, 294   see Emotion, Hate
Luck, 302   see Fate,
    Opportunity
Lying, 303   see Hypocrisy

Man, 307   see Bachelor,
  Woman
Manners, 309
Marriage, 311   see Alimony,
  Divorce
Memory, 313
Mind, 314   see Thought
Money, 315   see Business,
  Taxes
Morality, 317   see Bible, God
Music, 318   see Arts

Neighbor, 320

Opinion, 322
Opportunity, 323   see Luck
Optimism, 324   see Hope
Originality, 325   see Creativity

Parents, 326   see Ancestry,
  Family
Patience, 328   see Character
Peace, 329   see War
Pleasure, 330   see Happiness,
  Joy
Politics, 332   see Conservative,
  Government, Liberal
Poverty, 334   see Riches
Power, 335
Praise, 337
Prejudice, 338   see Bigotry
Procrastination, 340

Reading, 340   see Authors,
  Books, Education, Literature,
  Words
Reality, 340
Reason, 343   see Insanity,
  Thought
Reputation, 344
Revenge, 345   see Hate
Riches, 346   see Success
Right, 350   see Virtue

Security, 351
Self, 352   see Ego

Sex, 354   see Love, Marriage
Silence, 355   see Talk
Sincerity, 356   see Hypocrisy
Solitude, 357   see Loneliness
Sorrow, 358   see Grief
Success, 359   see Confidence,
  Celebrity, Talent
Suffering, 361   see Grief,
  Sorrow

Talent, 363   see Acting, Film,
  Hollywood, Television
Talk, 364   see Silence
Taste, 365
Taxes, 366   see Business
Television, 367   see Acting,
  Hollywood
Temptation, 369
Thought, 370   see Reason
Time, 372   see Age
Travel, 373   see Journeys
Troubles, 374
Trust, 375   see Belief

Understanding, 376
Universe, 376   see World

Vanity, 377   see Ego
Vice, 379   see Crime, Evil,
  Virtue
Virtue, 380   see Crime, Evil

War, 382   see Fighting
Wife, 383   see Husband,
  Marriage
Wisdom, 384
Woman, 386   see Man,
  Marriage
Words, 389   see Author, Books,
  Education, Learning,
  Literature
Work, 390   see Ambition,
  Success
World, 392   see Universe

Youth, 393   see Children

Index of Sources

Accius, Lucius 196
Acheson, Dean 171
Acts, Book of 270
Adams, Henry 125, 190
Addison, Joseph 261
Ade, George 146, 313
Adenauer, Konrad 154
Aeschylus 289, 361
Agathon 176
Agee, James 131
Aiken, Conrad 72
Aiken, George 339
Alain 47, 220
Alcott, Bronson 114, 228
Alexander, Cecil Francis 177
Alexander, Henry C. 348
Alger, Horatio 30
Alinsky, Saul 53
Allen, Fred 70, 84, 111, 112, 367
Allen, J. 66
Allen, Woody 100
Amiel, Henri 37, 190
Anaxandrides 97
Anderson, C. 53
Anderson, Maxwell 9
Anouilh, Jean 301
Antrim, Minna 271
Appleton, Thomas Gold 18
Arbuthnot, Jean 333
Aristophanes 20, 388
Aristotle 211, 270, 271, 380
Arnold, Matthew 231, 354
Arnold, Thurman 80
Atlee, Clement 105
Auden, W. H. 62, 306

Babson, Roger 109
Bacon, Francis 124, 165, 210, 250, 253, 254, 255, 270, 272, 288, 297, 310, 323, 345, 346, 353, 357, 380, 383, 384
Baer, Arthur 26
Bagehot, Walter 75, 92, 232
Baldwin, Faith 74
Baldwin, James 37, 72, 170
Baldwin, Stanley 154
Ball, Joseph 352
Balzac, Honoré de 6, 35, 133, 246, 268, 381
Barret-Booth 8
Barrie, James M. 75, 283
Barry, I. 156
Barrymore, John 26, 28, 121, 159
Barth, John 73
Barton, Bruce 85
Baruch, Bernard 89
Barzun, Jacques 231, 278
Basho, Matsuo 204
Battista, O.A. 321
Baudelaire, Charles 3, 285
Beard, P. 196
Beaumarchais, Pierre de 262, 360
Beauvoir, Simone de 80, 387
Beckford, William 200
Bede (Venerable) 282
Beecher, Henry Ward 31, 70, 187, 195, 200
Beerbohm, Max 132, 234
Behrman, S. N. 208
Belloc, Hilaire 62, 305

398

Ben Eleazer, Rabbi 167
Ben Gurion, David 238
Benchley, Nathaniel 37
Benchley, Robert 96
Benét, Stephen 60
Bennet, William 73
Bennett, Arnold 21, 39, 64, 247
Beranger, Pierre 263
Berlin, Irving 360
Bernanos, Georges 200
Bernard, Claude 36
Bernard, Tristan 235
Bibesco, Elizabeth 168, 169, 211
Bierce, Ambrose 1, 49, 88, 96, 142, 148, 174, 191, 207, 255, 260, 275, 279, 324, 333, 387
Billinger, S. 175
Billings, Josh 102, 116, 119, 198, 217, 288, 305, 334, 358
Bishop, Jim 171
Bismarck, Otto von 202
Blackfeet Indians 288
Blake, William 10, 58, 108, 124, 133, 168, 178, 213, 266, 287, 392
Blanchard, Paul 82
Bok, Derek 22, 272
Book of Common Prayer, The 329, 341, 392
Boorstin, S. 60
Bottome, Paul 73
Bourdaloue, Louis 299
Bovee, C. N. 251
Bowen, Elizabeth 203
Brando, Marlon 121
Brecht, Bertolt 159
Brenan, Gerald 22, 61, 93
Brese 46
Breton, André 260
Brian, E. 290
Briand, Aristide 352
Brillat-Savarin, Anthelme 110, 160
Brooks, Van Wyck 93
Browne, Sir Thomas 226, 283, 284, 343, 379, 392

Browning, Elizabeth Barrett 295
Browning, Robert 17, 21, 73, 220, 350
Bruce, Lenny 24, 267, 278
Bruder, C. 86
Buchan, John 103
Buddha 74
Bulwer-Lytton, Edward 96, 129, 278, 296
Bunche, Ralph 155
Burdon, Eric 81, 94
Burgess, Gelett 393
Burke, Edmund 110, 235, 310
Burns, George 71
Burns, Robert 294, 308
Burr, Aaron 340
Burroughs, John 67
Burton, Robert 234, 308, 315, 327, 334, 359, 383, 390
Butler, Samuel 1, 33, 104, 109, 136, 179, 204, 216, 224, 283, 288, 300, 304, 322, 323, 352, 353, 380

Cabell, James Branch 313, 325
Calderón 336
Campbell, Thomas 325
Camus, Albert 230, 248, 351, 354, 358
Canete, Manuel 203
Canetti, Elias 60, 163
Cantor, Eddie 95
Caplan, Mortimer 366
Capote, Truman 196
Carlyle, Thomas 6, 81, 189, 227, 252, 258, 262, 264, 288, 356, 390
Carnegie, Andrew 348
Carrel, Alexis 362
Carroll, Lewis 62, 246, 281, 354, 389
Carson, Rachel 250
Casanova 212
Castle, William R. 320
Cather, Willa 250, 363
Caxton, William 297

Cernuda, Luis 44
Cervantes, Miguel de 69, 99, 225, 269, 295, 302
Chamberlain, Neville 330
Chamfort, Nicolas 44, 118, 135, 200, 235, 263, 285
Chanel, Coco 72
Channing, Carol 264
Chapin, E. 92
Chapman, John Jay 127
Chardonne, Jacques 275
Charles II 159
Chateaubriand, François René de 77
Chaucer, Geoffrey 19, 261, 280, 294, 295, 372
Chazal, M. 36, 57, 104, 159
Chekhov, Anton 113, 191, 271, 293
Cher 19
Chesterton, G. K. 49, 59, 98, 122, 137, 141, 142, 149, 150, 237, 258, 265
Chevalier, Maurice 19
Chuang-Tzu 256
Churchill, Charles 365
Churchill, Winston 25, 92, 112, 257, 305
Cibber, Colley, 370
Cicero 21, 61, 107, 190, 274, 309, 331, 353, 371, 375
Clarke, John 297
Clarke, Tom 80
Clay, Henry 350
Clemenceau, Georges 155
Cleveland, Grover 106
Cobbett, William 335
Cocteau, Jean 59, 157
Colbert, Jean Baptiste 366
Coleman, George, the Elder 384
Coleridge, Samuel 174, 294, 337, 363
Collie, G. Norman 216
Collier, David 59
Collins, John Churton 169
Colton, Charles Caleb 224, 229
Columbat 257

Confucius 33, 199, 251, 284, 320
Congreve, William 319
Connolly, Cyril 128, 151, 220, 342
Connolly, James Brendan 190
Conrad, Joseph 12, 26, 109, 136
Coolidge, Calvin 67
Cooper, Anthony Ashley 310
Corinthians, First Book of 309, 313
Corinthians, Second Book of 276
Cornfeld, Bernard 44
Coven, Arnold 106
Coward, Noel 263
Cowley, Abraham 283
Cowley, Hannah 261, 378, 386
Cowper, William 224, 346, 350
Crane, Frank 103, 212
Crisp, Quentin 172
Cumming, E. 52
Cummings, E. E. 377
Curtis, Charles 51

Da Vinci, Leonardo 101, 210
Dac, P. 172
Daedalus 73
Dane, F. 130, 277
Danze, L. 94
Darling, Charles John 266
Darrow, Clarence 143, 284
DeForest, Lee 368
De Gaulle, Charles 22, 333
De Marquis 221
De Mille, Cecil B. 112
De Musset, Alfred 139
De Rieux 278
De Saint-Real 198
Defoe, Daniel 249
Dekker, Thomas, 214, 295
Demetrius 193
Democritus 108, 167
Depew, Chauncey 324
Descartes, René 238, 371
Deshoulieres 255
Dhammapada, The 264
Di Cavour, O. 112

Dickinson, Emily 17, 68, 75
Diderot, Denis 180
Dillon, William 327
Diogenes 291
Disney, Walt 60
Disraeli, Benjamin 39, 81, 113, 186, 194, 284, 328, 332, 393, 394
Djilas, Milovan 170
Donne, John 109
Dostoyevsky, Feodor 91, 217, 358
Douglas, Norman 14, 249, 272
Draxe, Thomas 213, 346
Dressler, Marie 208
Drucker, Peter 123, 241
Dryden, John 63, 240, 296, 328, 380, 382
Dr. Johnson; *see* Johnson, Samuel
Duclos, Charles Pinot 186
Dumahel, G. 179
Dumas, Alexandre, *fils* 180
Dumas, Alexandre, *père* 360, 385, 389
Dunne, Finley Peter 41, 114, 123, 148, 304
Durant, Will 146

Ecclesiastes, Book of 316, 378
Ecclesiasticus, Book of 274
Ehrlich, Paul 80
Einstein, Albert 83, 172, 285
Eisenhower, Dwight 28, 352
Eliot, George 85, 228
Eliot, T. S. 35, 101, 245, 342, 370
Ellis, Havelock, 176, 288
Ellsberg, Daniel 9
Emerson, Ralph Waldo 3, 7, 18, 19, 62, 65, 73, 77, 87, 88, 109, 167, 175, 176, 177, 182, 192, 207, 221, 227, 235, 242, 271, 290, 299, 311, 323, 349, 352, 363, 371, 373
Emerson, Robert 162
Ephesians, Book of 213

Epictetus 55, 89, 178
Epicurus 166
Erasmus 154, 330
Estienne, Henri 20
Etherege, Sir George 298
Euripides 168, 248, 337, 371, 393
Ewart, Gavin 136

Farrell, Joseph 116
Faulkner, William 40, 68, 298
Feather, William 22, 251
Feiffer, Jules 143
Feinberg, Abraham 200
Feldman, Marty 263
Fielding, Henry 135, 375
Fields, W. C. 8, 232, 348
Filene, Edward 123
FitzGerald, Edward 371
Fitzgerald, F. Scott 345, 347
Flaubert, Gustave 36, 204
Flavel, John 50
Fletcher, John 280
Florian, Jean Pierre 337
Florio, John 334
Fontenelle, Bernard 206
Ford, Henry 95
Forester, C. S. 58
Forster, E. M. 260, 319
Fort, Paul 17
Fosdick, Harry Emerson 22, 81, 106, 178
Fouché, Joseph 95
France, Anatole 60, 67, 104, 108, 179, 205, 225, 257, 267, 353
Frank, Anne 194
Franklin, Benjamin 66, 118, 124, 126, 144, 166, 181, 201, 216, 259, 279, 306, 331, 343, 351, 360, 367, 382, 388
Freud, Sigmund 183, 224
Frisch, Max 140
Fromm, Eric 129, 172
Frost, Robert 27, 28, 111, 161, 266, 321
Fuller, Buckminster 377

401

Fuller, Robert 77
Fuller, Thomas 54, 55, 65, 97, 101, 137, 143, 196, 214, 215, 225, 244, 266, 270, 313, 335, 337, 375
Fuller, Thomas (II) 206

Gable, Clark 301
Gabor, Zsa Zsa 215, 301
Gallup, George 143
Galsworthy, John 57, 65, 97, 219
Gandhi, Mahatma 87, 93, 278
Garfield, James 90
Gassert, O. 57
Genesis, Book of 308, 357, 358
George, Henry, 334
Gibbon, Edward 116, 345
Gibran, Kahlil 5, 43, 55, 108, 128, 130, 133, 143, 144, 175, 176, 199, 229, 244, 271, 284
Gibson, Herbert 154
Gide, André 9, 59, 73, 339
Gilbert, William 126
Gilbert, W. S. 281, 283, 350, 364, 366
Ginsberg, Allen 315
Giono, Jean 64
Gish, Lillian 193
Gissing, George 118
Glasgow, A. 199
Godard, Jean-Luc 156, 157
Goethe, Johann Wolfgang von 2, 5, 61, 77, 103, 122, 128, 197, 206, 222, 227, 233, 234, 256, 263, 284
Goldoni, Carlo 57
Goldsmith, Oliver 116, 265, 274, 306, 331
Goldwater, Barry 277
Goldwyn, Samuel 156, 157, 208
Goodman, Benny 339
Goodman, Paul 93
Gould, Lawrence 351
Gourmont, Remy de 43, 76
Gracian, Baltasar 3, 42, 114, 139, 188, 234, 264

Graham, Martha 199
Grandma Moses 36
Grass, Günther 36, 106
Gray, Thomas 227
Greeley, Horace 49
Green, J. 65
Gregory, Dick 53, 277
Grenfell, J. 194
Greville, Richard Fulke 235
Guedalla, Philip 204
Guinou, Albert 230
Guiterman, Arthur 389
Gypsy Rose Lee 30

Hackett, Buddy 111
Haldane, J. B. S. 171
Halifax, Lord 2, 31, 47, 122, 210, 211
Hall, James 304
Hammarskjold, Dag 47
Hampton, Lionel 187
Hand, Edward 1
Harding, D. W. 35
Hardy, Thomas 211, 281, 329
Harris, Sydney J. 347
Harrol, Stewart 84
Hawthorne, Nathaniel 30, 98, 182, 260
Hayakawa, S. I. 141
Hazlitt, William 47, 51, 54, 101, 133, 137, 149, 204, 270, 279, 307, 331, 338, 353, 355, 365
Hebbel, Friederich 259
Hecht, Ben 29, 36, 99, 339
Hedges, J. 240
Heine, Heinrich 178, 252, 258
Heinlein, Robert 283, 289
Heller, Friedrich 205
Helps, Sir Arthur 251
Hemingway, Ernest 201, 233, 317
Henley, William Ernest 65
Henry, O. 285
Hepburn, Katharine 7, 10
Heraclitus 58, 71
Herbert, George 103, 166, 192, 218, 262, 270, 298, 320

Herodotus 203, 374
Herold, D. 236
Herold, J. Christopher 303, 317
Herolde, Don 139
Herrick, Robert 22, 285, 383
Hesse, Hermann 192, 243
Heywood, Thomas 330
Hippocrates 119, 280
Hitchcock, Alfred 7, 156
Hitler, Adolf 52, 307
Hobbes, John Oliver 219
Hobbes, Thomas 274
Hoffenstein, Samuel 354
Hoffer, Eric 128, 152, 163, 235
Hofmannsthal, Hugo von 256
Holmes, Oliver Wendell 4, 18,
    51, 78, 142, 145, 169, 215,
    228, 235, 304
Holmes, Oliver Wendell, Jr.
    189, 336
Homer 242, 384
Hooper, Ellen Sturgis 282
Hoover, Herbert 102, 187
Hope, Bob 81, 226, 238
Hopkins, Gerard Manley 385
Horace 15, 100, 255, 346, 349
Hoskins, Henry 9, 66, 223, 255,
    289
Housman, A. E. 303
Howe, E. W. 5, 15, 31, 42, 107,
    130, 158, 215
Howe, Joseph 188
Howe, Louis McHenry 333
Howell, James 344, 390
Hubbard, Elbert 2, 5, 84, 116,
    130, 140, 165, 174, 190, 191,
    276
Hubbard, Kin 42, 94, 150, 223,
    291, 335, 386
Hughes, J. 238
Hughes, Thomas 282
Hugo, Victor 20, 89, 170, 296,
    344
Hume, David 137
Humphrey, Hubert H. 321
Huneker, James Gibbons 215
Hunt, Leigh 388

Huntington, Collis P. 67
Huxley, Aldous 37, 76, 138,
    259, 292, 308, 331, 360, 363
Huxley, Thomas Henry 48, 50,
    253, 317, 385, 392

Ibn-Abi-Talib, Ali 205
Ibsen, Henrik 376
Ickes, Harold L. 96
Inge, William R. 193, 239
Ingersoll, Robert 31, 50, 176
Irvine, S. 155
Irving, Washington 188
Isaac 114

Jackson, Andrew 49
Jackson, Helen Hunt 182
Jacobs, Joe 150
Jacques, Jules 182
James, Henry 248
James, William 55, 138, 153,
    194, 309
Janin, Jules Gabriel 151
Jarrell, Randall 206
Jeans, Sir James 377
Jefferson, Thomas 14, 173, 267,
    279, 348
Jenyns, Soame 81
Jerome, Jerome K. 223, 244,
    269, 286
Job, Book of 280, 372, 374, 385,
    389
John, Gospel According to 197,
    298
Johnson, Samuel 3, 4, 22, 37,
    46, 51, 68, 76, 79, 99, 117,
    125, 137, 145, 153, 157, 160,
    169, 188, 210, 211, 214, 218,
    220, 223, 224, 226, 227, 229,
    236, 244, 245, 249, 253, 254,
    273, 286, 292, 297, 303, 310,
    312, 313, 318, 327, 331, 334,
    335, 336, 341, 352, 373, 375,
    379, 381, 392
Jones, Franklin P. 131, 148, 320
Jones, T. 197
Jonson, Ben 226, 327, 345, 364
Joubert, Joseph 39, 48, 76

INDEX

Joubert, Petrus Jacobus 142
Jowett, Benjamin 149
Joyce, James 281
Jung, Carl 101, 222, 229, 256
Juvenal 192, 314
Juvenal, Bertrand de 95

Kafka, Franz 180, 243
Kant, Immanuel 10
Kaufman, Lionel 78
Keaton, Buster 264
Keats, John 16, 246, 253
Keller, Helen 27, 30, 55, 56
Kelly, Walt 130
Kempis, Thomas à; see Thomas
 à Kempis
Kennedy, John F. 94, 140, 155,
 164, 364
Kenyatta, Jomo 178
Kerouac, Jack 183
Kettering, Charles F. 173
Key, Thomas Hewitt 314
Keynes, John Maynard 220
Khayyam, Omar 150, 280
Kierkegaard, Sören 82, 121,
 181, 221, 274, 285
King, Martin Luther, Jr. 53, 101
Kingsley, Charles 391
Kipling, Rudyard 22, 387, 389
Kirk, Lisa 364
Kissinger, Henry 10, 205
Koestler, Arthur 183, 264
Koretser Rabbi, The 179
Kozinski, Jerzy 140
Kraus, Karl 256
Kraus, L. 258

LaBiche, Eugène 305
La Bruyère, Jean de 56, 100,
 158, 182, 214, 247, 262, 287
La Follette, Robert 231
La Fontaine, Jean de 304
La Guardia, Fiorello H. 233
Laing, R. D. 151
Lamartine, Alphonse de 330
Lamb, Arthur J. 312
Lamb, Charles 114, 326, 341,
 346

Landor, Walter Savage 377
Langbridge, Frederick 325
Langland, William 326
Lao-tse 251
Lardner, Ring 147
La Rochefoucauld, François de
 11, 16, 54, 57, 89, 97, 102,
 107, 132, 136, 153, 157, 158,
 162, 165, 169, 188, 190, 193,
 198, 210, 217, 222, 239, 247,
 268, 299, 338, 356, 357, 364,
 378, 379, 381, 388
La Sale, Antoine de 296
Lavater, Johann 162
Lawrence, D. H. 61, 256
Lawrence, T. E. 195
Leacock, Stephen 14, 291
Leary, Timothy 68
Lebowitz, Fran 79, 125
Lec, Stanislaw 22, 181
Leigh, Vivien 43
Lemmon, Jack 79
Lemontey 302
L'Enclos, Ninon de 43, 76
Lennon, John 181
Leopardi, Giacomo 134
Lessing, Doris 262
Levant, Oscar 126
Levinson, Sam 231, 233
Leviticus, Book of 320
Lewis, C. S. 62
Lewis, Joe E. 24, 25, 33, 111,
 347
Lewis, Sinclair 28, 124
Lewis, Sir George Cornwall 332
Lichtenberg, Georg Christoph
 3, 48, 59, 121, 140, 174, 202,
 222
Lieberman, Irv 367
Lillie, Beatrice 367
Lincoln, Abraham 29, 69, 90,
 104, 129, 192, 350
Linkletter, Art 77
Lippman, Walter 48, 89
Livy 195
Locke, John 220, 314, 341, 371
Lois, George 94
London, L. 113

Longfellow, Henry Wadsworth 6, 281, 319, 328, 362
Lord Acton 335
Lord Byron 64, 78, 92, 166, 197, 239, 245, 246, 254, 262, 312, 316, 345, 348
Lord Chesterfield 217, 269, 341, 384
Lord Dunsany 171
Lord Halifax 144, 272
Lord Mansfield 249
Lord Rochester 78
Loren, Sophia 44
Lorimer, George Claude 193
Lovelace, Richard 298
Lowell, James Russell 327
Lowell, John 105
Lubbock, John 274
Luke, Book of 329, 344
Luther, Martin, 12, 142, 354

Macaulay, Thomas Babington 317
Machiavelli, Niccolò 351, 359
MacLeish, Archibald 183
Magritte, René 152
Mankiewicz, Herbert 207
Mann, Thomas 99, 155
Manuel, Eugene 158
Manville, Tommy 26, 183
Mao Zedong 155
Marcus Aurelius 32
Mark, Gospel According to 369
Mark, Robert 266
Marlowe, Christopher 296
Marquis, Don 20, 27, 324, 340
Martial 70, 145, 261
Marx, Groucho 24, 38
Marx, Karl 200, 219
Marx, Sam 207, 208
Masefield, John 283
Massinger, Philip 328
Masson, Tom 15
Matthew, Gospel According to 46, 247, 349, 369
Maugham, W. Somerset 131, 171, 316, 361
Maxwell, Elsa 263

Mayer, Louis B. 208
McLaughlin, M. 87, 299
Mead, Margaret 146
Meir, Golda 238, 239
Melville, Herman 163
Menander 310, 387
Mencken, H. L. 23, 33, 40, 52, 58, 71, 85, 88, 105, 169, 202, 218, 249, 252, 257, 280, 293, 295, 300, 305, 318, 333, 335, 344, 355
Mendel of Kotzk 179
Meninger, William 11
Menninger, Karl 237
Meredith, George 118
Metternich, Klemens von 131
Midler, Bette 40
Milhaud, J. 98
Mill, John Stuart 325
Millay, Edna St. Vincent 99, 287
Miller, Henry 74, 342
Miller, Joaquin 347
Miller, L. 63
Milne, A. A. 39
Milton, John 12, 259, 293, 314, 319, 322, 329, 330, 357
Mitford, Nancy 79
Mizner, Wilson 9, 90, 201
Molière 56, 136, 379
Monroe, Vaughan 123
Montagu, Lady Mary Wortley 310
Montague, Ashley 22, 128
Montaigne, Michel de 52, 69, 76, 86, 100, 161, 213, 216, 225, 248, 296, 308, 309, 355
Montesquieu, Baron de 61, 82, 163, 191, 194, 236, 272, 359
Montherlant, Henry de 205
Moore, George 27, 244, 378
Moore, Mary Tyler 34
Moore, Thomas 294
Morgenstern, Christian 34
Morley, Christopher 44, 87, 154, 276
Morley, John 98
Morton, Thomas 328
Mother Theresa 184

Muggeridge, Malcolm 184
Mumford, Ethel 146
Musset, Alfred de 232

Napoleon 2, 177, 213
Nash, Ogden 45, 303, 326, 375, 377
Navik, J. 199
Newman, John Henry Cardinal 135, 253, 289
Newton, Howard 283
Nicholson, Jack 8
Nietzsche, Friedrich Wilhelm 35, 48, 68, 78, 92, 123, 126, 132, 144, 146, 154, 167, 178, 203, 219, 272, 276, 304, 305, 336, 361, 378, 387
Nin, Anaïs 75, 299
Nixon, Richard M. 368
Nodier, Charles 300
Norris, Kathleen 285

Ogilvie, H. 268
Oldenburg, Klaus 11
Olivier, Laurence 8
O'Malley, Frank Ward 287
Orwell, George 14, 33, 163, 206, 221
Osler, William 119, 143, 260
Ottis, James 366
Overbury, Sir Thomas, 306
Ovid 30, 150, 294, 297, 320, 330, 343, 372

Paine, Thomas 164, 227
Parker, Dorothy 79, 129, 264
Parkinson, C. Northcote 391
Parrish, Anne 185
Pascal, Blaise 4, 217, 237, 259, 275, 343
Pasteur, Louis 241
Pavese, Cesare 196
Peirce, Charles S. 318
Penn, William 15, 183, 196, 361
Pepys, Samuel 316
Pericles 159
Phelps, William Lyon 49, 236
Philippians, Book of 329
Phillips, Wendell, 102

Phocylides 315
Pindar 242
Pitt, William 267, 336
Plato 91, 289, 354, 380
Pliny the Elder 25, 280, 291
Plutarch 387
Polanski, Roman 156
Pope, Alexander 51, 127, 161, 209, 237, 250, 265, 269, 306, 319, 322, 337, 338
Pope John XXIII 24
Pope Leo XIII 362
Pope Paul VI 170
Pound, Ezra 39, 292
Prentice, George 38, 102
Prince Charles 10
Prochnow, Herbert 13, 21, 42, 83, 124, 189, 226, 278
Proudhon, Pierre Joseph 70
Proust, Marcel 59, 71, 134, 153, 191, 204, 209, 221
Proverbs, Book of 175, 253, 346, 376, 383
Psalms, Books of 18, 245, 279, 385
Publilius Syrus 127, 137, 138, 376

Quillen, Robert 116

Rabelais, François 99, 365
Rand, Edward 202
Raper, John 223
Ray, John 214, 301, 383
Ray, Man 93, 141
Reagan, Nancy 386
Renard, Jules 17, 38, 133, 232
Ricard, Louis Xavier de 386
Richardson, Ralph 260
Richter, Jean Paul 197, 251, 359
Ridley, E. 41
Rigaut, Jacques 17
Rilke, Rainer Maria 301
Rinehart, Mary Roberts 157, 362
Rivarol, Antoine de 5
Rockne, Knute 339
Rodgers & Hammerstein 110

INDEX

Rodin, Auguste 83
Rogers, Samuel 20, 302, 311
Rogers, Will 14, 30, 67, 201, 202, 212, 233
Romulo, Carlos P. 112
Roosevelt, Eleanor 153, 289
Roosevelt, Franklin D. 88, 151
Roosevelt, Theodore 4, 123, 186
Roper, John 117, 223
Rorem, Ned 232
Rosenzweig, Franz 179, 180
Rostand, Jean 22, 138, 145, 219
Rouchard, H. 241
Rowland, Helen 41, 42, 111, 117, 216, 252, 275
Rowley, William 323
Rozanov, V. V. 182
Ruskin, John 43, 66, 85, 125, 365
Russell, Bertrand 10, 79, 82, 152, 266, 273, 343
Rutherford 100

Sa'di 291
Salinger, J. D. 340
Sandburg, Carl 122
Santayana, George 13, 68, 115, 134, 148, 201, 207, 255, 279, 286, 314
Sarnoff, Robert 368
Sartre, Jean-Paul 260
Schenk, Nicholas M. 209
Schiller, Johann Friedrich von 267, 376
Schoenberg, Arnold 36
Schopenhauer, Arthur 17, 45, 62, 98, 99, 110, 120, 135, 152, 180, 205, 218, 223, 227, 236, 256
Schulberg, Budd 217
Schuster, W. 276
Scorsese, Martin 301
Scott, Howard 95
Scott, Sir Walter 25, 372
Scott, Zachary 24
Seeger, Pete 273
Selden, John 254, 258, 322, 331

Seldes, George 86
Seneca 95, 100, 108, 179, 374, 379
Seuss, Dr. 79
Sévigné, Marquise de 168
Shakespeare, William 12, 13, 41, 78, 97, 101, 106, 132, 145, 189, 212, 214, 240, 247, 280, 282, 291, 294, 297, 298, 308, 309, 310, 313, 314, 318, 323, 328, 338, 353, 358, 359, 361, 371, 372, 375, 381, 382, 388, 392, 393
Shaw, George Bernard 6, 29, 40, 61, 72, 73, 90, 118, 120, 131, 135, 149, 158, 159, 173, 193, 201, 206, 212, 231, 241, 242, 243, 295, 311, 312, 316, 318, 326, 344, 347, 357, 366, 370, 380, 387, 393
Shaw, Herbert 27
Sheen, Fulton J. 181
Sheffield, John 176
Shelley, Percy Bysshe 214, 252, 337, 371
Shenstone, William 32, 305
Sheridan, Richard Brinsley 248, 365
Shoaff, Edgar 13
Sidney, Sir Philip 383
Simenon, Georges 40
Simon, Paul 117
Simpson, Wallis Warfield 347
Singer, Isaac Bashevis 181
Smith, Al 28
Smith, Edgar 391
Smith, Lillian 203
Smith, Logan Pearsall 63, 168, 218, 287, 312, 315, 340, 341
Smith, Roy 248
Smith, Sydney 91, 141, 166, 277
Smith, W. 302
Socrates 41, 74, 108, 122, 160, 185, 187
Solomon, Song of 240, 295
Solon 194
Sophocles 151, 308
South, Robert 258

Southerland, D. 237
Southerne, Thomas 345
Souvestre 70, 225
Spencer, Herbert 43, 83, 322
Spenser, Edmund 261, 310, 372
Spinoza, Baruch 16, 152, 271, 356
Springsteen, Bruce 289
Spurgeon, Charles 50
Staël, Madame de 376
Steiger, Rod 74, 184, 258
Stein, Gertrude 271
Steinem, Gloria 272
Stephen, J. F. 325
Stephens, James 176
Stern, Judith 139
Stevens, Wallace 35, 228
Stevenson, Adlai 10, 22, 109, 164, 186, 187
Stevenson, Robert Louis 66, 152, 166, 281, 290, 307, 373, 374
Stimson, Henry L. 210
Stoppard, Tom 22, 106
Strachey, Lytton 69
Stravinsky, Igor 35, 171
St. Augustine 76
St. Beuve, Charles Augustin 145
St. Clement 210
Saint-Gaudens, Augustus 34
St. Prosper 299
Sudermann, Hermann 262, 291
Sunday, Billy 50
Surtees, R. S. 332, 384
Sutherland, George 164
Sutton, D. 78, 286
Swetchine, Anne Sophie 21
Swift, Jonathan 18, 20, 50, 70, 114, 125, 136, 174, 192, 203, 266, 303, 370, 393
Szasz, Thomas 80, 115, 230

Tacitus 54, 336
Talleyrand-Perigord, Charles Maurice de 166
Talmud 21, 180
Tawney, R. H. 203, 324

Teasdale, Sara 246
Tennyson, Alfred Lord 110, 168, 228, 306, 373
Terence 355
Teshigahara, S. 45
Thackeray, William Makepeace 312, 332
Thalberg, Irving 208
Thomas à Kempis 179
Thompson, Dorothy 343
Thoreau, Henry David 7, 47, 60, 72, 74, 138, 141, 170, 185, 191, 230, 234, 243, 270, 282, 292, 358, 373, 385
Thorek, M. 198
Thurber, James 33, 39, 242, 355, 386
Tierney, Father H. B. 321
Tillich, Paul 147, 184
Tillotson, John 336
Timothy, First Book of 315
Tocqueville, Alexis de 1
Toklas, Alice B. 19
Tolstoy, Leo 85, 147, 378
Townsend, Lynn A. 339
Toynbee, Arnold 28, 71
Tracy, Spencer 7
Trudeau, Pierre Elliott 321
Truman, Harry 16, 200
Tupamaros 259
Twain, Mark 18, 19, 27, 31, 45, 56, 63, 68, 86, 89, 115, 120, 123, 124, 132, 147, 159, 160, 165, 167, 173, 185, 225, 241, 255, 304, 311, 319, 350, 363, 369, 381, 391

Unamuno, Miguel de 142
Ustinov, Peter 263

Valéry, Paul 1, 34, 178, 181, 198, 221, 222
Van Loon, Hendrik Willem 84
Vanbrugh, Sir John 388
Vaperean, J. 98
Vare, Daniele 112
Vaughn, Billy 32

Vauvenargues, Marquis de 4, 47, 64, 135, 137, 209, 268, 270, 370
Veblen, Thorstein 14
Virgil 1
VOGUE Magazine 84
Voltaire 33, 51, 52, 54, 119, 130, 167, 169, 198, 228, 290, 339, 346, 358, 390

Walker, James J. 296
Wallace, William Ross 327
Walpole, Horace 121, 381
Walsh, Dariel 321
Walsh, H. 67
Warburg, J. 89
Warhol, Andy 35
Warner, Charles Dudley 333
Washington, Booker T. 6, 53
Washington, George, 382
Waugh, Evelyn, 64
Wayne, John 53
Webster, Daniel 97
Weil, Simone 32, 184
Welles, Orson 105, 156, 368
Wells, H. G. 14, 83, 240, 302, 318
Wesley, John 338
West, Mae 135, 212, 300
West, Rebecca 36
Westcott, Edward Noyes 120
Wharton, Edith 356
Whately, Richard 386
Whistler, James McNeill 34
White, E. B. 38, 355
Whitehead, Alfred North 46, 317
Whitehorn, Katherine 64
Whittier, John Greenleaf 113
Wilcox, Ella Wheeler 262

Wilde, Oscar 11, 15, 18, 21, 29, 30, 36, 41, 44, 46, 48, 54, 59, 77, 88, 91, 95, 99, 106, 116, 126, 127, 129, 139, 147, 148, 149, 172, 173, 174, 175, 204, 209, 215, 217, 226, 236, 240, 242, 245, 250, 261, 271, 274, 276, 282, 287, 291, 295, 300, 302, 306, 307, 312, 326, 332, 356, 362, 369
Wilder, Thornton 292
Wilding, Michael 8
Williams, Tennessee 164
Williams, William Carlos 104
Wilson, Earl 156
Wilson, Woodrow 29, 63, 71, 105, 186, 202
Winchell, Walter 165, 371
Wittgenstein, Ludwig 259
Wolfe, Thomas 293
Wonder, Stevie 287
Woolf, Virginia 206
Woollcott, Alexander 332
Wordsworth, William 11, 250, 293, 342, 359
Wright, Frank Lloyd 43
Wyat, W. 301
Wylie, Max 362
Wylie, Philip 327

Xenophanes 177, 189

Yankowich, Leon 146
Yeats, William Butler 25, 60
Yevtushenko, Yevgeny 265
Young, Edward 56, 340
Yukichi 5

Zegri, Amando 246
Zero, J. 64